HOW'D that FOOT GET iN my MOUTH?

(Reflections of a life-long flibbertigibbet)

by

BiLL RuSSeLL

How'd That Foot Get in My Mouth?
Copyright © 2015 by Bill Russell.

ISBN Number 0-692380-30-2

Written and designed by Bill Russell.

For other titles by Bill Russell, see the back pages of this book.

Dedication

To my sainted mother. I'll never know how she put up with me. I suspect it has a lot to do with feminine curiosity... Ditto goes for my wife, Norelle. I suspect she just wants to see what I'll do next.

ACKNOWLedgeMeNtS

I'm indebted to the nice folks who run The Plainsman newspaper here in Huron, South Dakota. In particular, my thanks to Crystal Pugsley who first thought this stuff might be worth reading.

STORY LISTINGS

The stories in this collection are in
random, rather than chronological order.

1
ReFLectioNS

During my life, I never knew a time when I didn't have electric lights, indoor plumbing, a refrigerator, telephone, newspapers, magazines, movies, records, and automobiles. Later came television, VCRs, air conditioning, computers, email and social networking. On the radio, we listened to dramas like *I Love a Mystery*, *Inner Sanctum*, *The Green Hornet* and *Gang Busters*. For comedy, I couldn't wait for *Henry Aldrich*, *The Life of Reilly* and *Our Miss Brooks*. When TV came along we tuned in to *Gunsmoke*, *Playhouse 90*, *Abbot and Costello*, *Have Gun Will Travel* and *Death Valley Days*. It's hard now to remember a time without 'the tube' standing in the corner of the room. My brother, some years back, was explaining to his daughter (age eight), how tough we had it as children. "Vickie," he said, "when your uncle Bill and I were kids, we didn't have television so we had to listen to stories on the radio." She tussled with the concept for a few moments and asked this very logical question, "What did you do with your eyes?" Times change.

I've been fortunate enough to have flown in an airplane, cruised on a ship, traveled cross-country by car, train and bus, and watched a man rocket from the earth and land on the moon. We also gazed in awe as a man in a rocket-powered airplane broke a barrier very few knew existed – sound. All these things our ancestors would have found jaw-dropping and yet we just accepted such phenomena as normal, even as owed to us.

When I was sick, there were hospitals with x-rays, penicillin, and delicate scientific surgeries by people who knew what they were doing. Gone were the days of bleeding a patient in a barbershop. (Did you know that is where the barber pole came from? Barbers, who were also bleeding practitioners in the Middle Ages, used to advertise by wrapping a bloody rag around a pole in order to attract customers. Think of it, you could get a nice shave, have your ears lowered and bleed your bad spirits out all at the same time. Thank Heaven for the AMA!)

I've always had access to modern schools, although my scholastic output was, no doubt, very disappointing to my parents and teachers. I even dabbled in higher education, briefly. I think I got bored easily or perhaps it was just laziness. That's a far more likely scenario. I just couldn't waste my valuable playtime on anything as mundane as study. I was a little better in college, but not much. Playtime still came first. Somehow, through the years and in spite of my best efforts, I learned to read, write, and add numbers which, even today, amazes me. Thank you, my teachers, for sticking it out. I'd have probably given up on me a long time ago. Maybe that's why I never became a teacher, I was afraid I'd have to put up with someone like me!

Now that it's much closer to the end than the beginning, I have time to reflect and the inescapable conclusion I've come to is this: I'd love to do it all over again and I wouldn't change anything. What the heck, it was a lot of fun. The marvelous part is that through it all I have loved and been loved and felt the joy of devotion to another and the warmth of devotion bestowed on me, some of which you'll see in the stories that follow…

2

Duchess and the Wax Build-Up

In the winter of 1947, my brother Dave and I received a stupendous present: a marvelous dog named Duchess. A cross between a German shepherd and a collie, she was nine months old and still wearing a bandage around her middle from having been recently spayed. I don't remember who we got her from. I guess it doesn't matter except I'd love to thank them over and over for this very special gift. Even though we had a rocky start, Duchess became our best friend, our buddy and constant companion through our growing up years. To this day, she is the standard by which I measure all other dogs. On that first night, however, it was touch and go. She slept on the floor between our beds. It was winter, as wintry as it gets in San Diego on the beach, but we opened the window wide and tried to sleep with the covers pulled over our heads. The foul atmosphere created by our new friend left us no alternative. I have no idea what that dog had been eating before we got her but each time she tooted, a ghastly odor permeated the room – the kind that can cause paint to peel and wallpaper to sag.

Throughout the night, muffled cries of, "Ugh, ah, that's awful. Come on dog, stop it!" could be heard. Even hunkering down under the covers or standing by the window did not guaranty a breath of fresh air. Of course, being eleven and twelve, we sniggered the entire time. It was during that period of development when bodily functions are giggle-worthy. Each time the uproar occurred, Duchess jumped up and came, with her tail wagging, to each of us to see what the excitement was about. She seemed immune to the atmosphere she'd created, just curious about the resulting chaos. In the wee small hours of the morning, the storm either passed or fatigue shut down our sense of smell. Whatever it was, we slept. That was our memorable introduction to this wonderful family treasure. In the weeks and months that followed she became our constant companion and faithful buddy.

One summer day, Mom gave Dave and me the chore of waxing the kitchen floor. I don't think it had ever been waxed before and we set about the task with vigor. That in itself was amazing since we were much more adept at shirking work than taking a hand in it. Using a couple of worn out socks, we applied a generous coating and while one sat in the middle of an old army blanket, the other pulled it around and around until the floor fairly glistened. Duchess watched but obviously bored after awhile, retired to her favorite spot at the dark end of the hall. The hall was sixteen feet long with a floor also covered in linoleum. If someone came to the kitchen door while she snoozed, the explosion of excitement could be heard throughout the house. She would scramble to her feet, yipping and barking, the clatter of her claws trying to gain traction on the linoleum like the sound of hail on a tin roof. Reaching the end of the hall in a blur of flailing legs and flashing paws, she would burst into the living room and when her feet hit the carpet, she went into hyper drive. Across the living room she bolted in three bounds, picking up speed with every stride. At the dining room door she didn't even slow down but made the turn with all four feet scrambling to find some traction, much like a race car in a tight turn. Then it was a beeline to the kitchen door where she skidded to a halt just inches short of slamming into the cabinets, all the time barking a clear warning to whoever it was that she was there.

After we'd finished waxing, Dave and I sat at the dining room table admiring our shiny floor. Johnny Peak, a friend from down the road came to the door. Johnny was like a brother and part of the family, he practically lived at our house. That didn't cut any mustard with Duchess. Everyone got the same greeting at the back door. When Johnny opened the door and stuck his head in, we heard her scramble to her feet and hitch it into high gear, yipping and barking. Gathering momentum, with all four feet slipping and sliding, she rattled down the hall and exploded into the living room, all legs flying. Hitting the carpet, she rocketed across the living room and entered the hairpin turn at the door to the kitchen, where she hit the freshly waxed floor. Her feet went out from under her and, legs flailing, she skidded across the room and plowed into the opposite wall. It was a scene from a *Roadrunner* cartoon. Wiley Coyote couldn't have done it better. As I sat watching her pass by, what struck me most was the disbelieving look on Duchess' face. A confused and bewildered look that said, *what-the-heck-happened?*

If nothing else, Duchess was a fast learner, and the next time someone came to the back door, I noticed she slowed down considerably approaching the kitchen and made an extremely wide turn. Dave and I toyed with the idea of waxing the hall too, but in the end decided that would be too cruel … besides, the novelty of housework had worn off by then.

3

DUCHESS AND THE NICOTINE FIT

In addition to living *at* the beach, my brother Dave and I almost lived *on* the beach, spending most of our summer days – early morning to the fading light – next to the water. Duchess made it a trio and Johnny Peak, our best friend, completed the quartet. It was interesting that, seemingly without any training, whenever Dave and I headed for the water, Duchess would appear and lie down next to our clothes. When we returned, she'd greet us and then it was off down the beach exploring. The moment we left again, there she'd be, back at her post. I didn't really think much about it, my thoughts taken up with girls, food and surfing at the time.

One morning I dialed Johnny's number, listened to the phone ring at the other end and heard a voice say, "Hello."

"Hey, you goin' to the beach?"

"Can't right now, I gotta finish cutting the lawn. I was supposed to do it yesterday and the ole man is pretty steamed so I'd better get it done. I'll be down later."

"Okay, see you there." I hung up. "Let's go, girl," I said to Duchess who had been watching the exchange and prancing around on the floor. She knew where we were going and didn't have much patience for all this last minute telephone chatter. Dave was already standing out front. Off we went with Duchess in the lead, merrily announcing our approach and checking out each and every favorite yard and alley along the route.

At the beach the waves looked inviting and, after stripping down to our bathing suits, Dave and I headed for the water. Duchess plopped down and put her head on her paws, ears at attention to await our return.

A half hour later, Johnny showed up and joined a bunch of school friends gathered further down the beach. He'd only been there ten minutes when he discovered he'd left his cigarettes at home. Unsuccessful at trying to bum one from the group, he thought he'd get one from us. Wrong!

He may have been like a brother and a constant fixture around our home, but ten feet was all the closer Duchess would let him get to our clothes. He had to return to the group empty handed. According to Johnny, she stood up bristling, daring him to move any closer. He decided he didn't want a smoke that bad. Fifteen minutes later, we came out of the water and Duchess greeted us. Johnny left the others and headed over. Before Duchess left on her explorations, she ran to him, wagging her tail and nuzzled his leg as if to say, 'No hard feelings, pal,' then she was off down the beach exploring and snooping. I guess she had her limits on what she'd tolerate and getting into our stuff when we weren't there was not something she was prepared to ignore.

4

Duchess Takes Charge

At a birthday party for my eight-year-old cousin Patty, the back yard was full of kids and you can imagine the noisy merriment. Duchess was right in the middle of the festivities. There were children from all over the neighborhood and classmates from school as well. That dog seemed to love throngs of kids around and mostly you'd find her wallowing right in the middle of 'em. Many is the time I'd walk into the backyard and see a pile of children on the lawn, laughing, yelling and squirming. I'd whistle and up she'd come, like a whale broaching the surface of the sea, shaking kids off like a duck shedding water. Her tolerance level was astounding – as long as she thought it was play. The afternoon of the party, the kids were all on the patio skylarking when one little boy cornered Patty and was flailing his arms and yelling. They were playing and she too was screaming with delight but Duchess must have thought it looked a bit too aggressive because I saw her come up behind the boy, gently take hold of the seat of his pants and pull him back a foot or two. Immediately things calmed down, to her satisfaction, and she took off to mingle with the others. I don't know if she'd do it for another child but Patty was family and to a German shepherd/collie, that automatically made her part of the litter.

As I recall while growing up, neighborhood dogs were free to roam, pretty much at will. Duchess had a friendly association with the two big dogs living next door. Trouble came when we inherited a Chow from a former neighbor who was going to work overseas and couldn't take the dog along. Mike was tough looking by any standard. He had a bushy mane, and a tuft of hair on the tip of his tail, but all the rest of his coat was gone. He lost it to some sort of skin condition and the effect was he looked just like a big red lion. Over the months, there were skirmishes with the dogs next door in which Mike did the fighting and Duchess circled the melee, barking encouragement, sort of a one-dog cheering section. The canine donnybrooks usually petered out when Dave or I pulled Mike out by the tail. However, one day things got out of hand and Mike was getting his clock cleaned. Duchess stepped in to help about the time I got there. She was a tiger, teeth flashing, snarling and bashing her way into the middle of the fray. I got Mike's tail and pulled him out, but Duchess was in a fighting frenzy by then and for several seconds seemed to have the situation under control. However, in the next instant, a quick glance around told her she had no backup. Mike wasn't there and she was in this thing alone. With a yelp and tail between her legs, she pulled out and took off up the road, the two Bishop dogs nipping at her heels. For a while though, she had been dishing it out real good. That's why I don't think Duchess was a coward, just very prudent.

After I got out of the Marines, I went to live with my sister and her husband in Lancaster, California. Duchess went with me. As a reward for landing my first real job, I bought a HiFi record player/radio/ tape recorder console (this was before stereo). One afternoon while Duchess was outside, I recorded myself calling to her. "Here, Duchess, here Duchess, come on girl, here Duchess." I erased everything from the tape five minutes ahead of the message and turned it off. Later, while she lay sleeping on the floor in the living room, I got up, went into the bedroom, turned on the tape, cranked the volume up, came back out and sat down. In five minutes the air was split by my voice calling. She jumped up and ran to the bedroom. In a few moments she appeared, looking rather sheepish, came over to me, rested her head on my knee for a second, then returned to her spot and flopped down.

About a week later, she was in her favorite spot once more and I decided to try it again. While she dozed, I went to the bedroom, started the tape, came back and sat down. When the noise came on, she raised her head, glanced around, saw me, looked toward the bedroom and flopped back down. It seems I couldn't fool the dog twice and I never tried again, she was too smart for that.

5

DUCHESS and the Hardest Thing I Ever Did

Do kids need dogs? Perhaps not, but what an empty world it would be without them. What better way for a child learn about loyalty, love, grief, sharing and responsibility than with a friend who asks nothing more in return than just to be with them? In late 1959, I took our buddy, Duchess, the dog my brother and I were raised with, to her veterinarian. By then she was failing and had begun a downward spiral. Less and less able to take care of herself, she spent most of her time sleeping in her favorite spot at the dark end of the hall. The normally fleecy white patches on her chest and neck had turned dingy grey and her whole coat looked musty and unkempt. Arthritis was making it difficult for her to get up or down, find a comfortable position or even move. Now in her twelfth year (eighty-fourth in dog years) she was a pitiful sight and it tore at my heart to see her in such a state.

I led her into the examining room and gently lifted her onto the table. She knew where she was and leaned against me. I could feel her slight shivering and I pulled her a bit closer.

"How's Miss Duchess today?" the voice behind me asked. Doc Kramer came into the room holding her charts. He patted her on the head and looked into her eyes. "I think her eyesight has probably gotten worse," he said, looking down at the chart. "What's the problem today?"

"Well, mostly she can't move and I know she's in a lot of pain."

He was silent for a few seconds, put his hand on Duchess's head, and said, "I've done just about all I can do for her in that department. If I increase her pain medicine, she'll turn into a vegetable and be of no use to anyone, let alone herself. It also looks like she's been losing weight. How's her appetite?"

"She doesn't seem very hungry lately, but she does eat, just not very much."

He stepped back, his eyes on Duchess and his head cocked. After a second he asked, his voice subdued to almost a whisper, "Have you thought about letting me put her to sleep?" He raised his hand when I stiffened. I must have had a horrified look on my face because he added, "I know, I know, that sounds mean and insensitive, but nature would have put her out of her misery long before she got to this age and it probably would have been by starvation, a cruel way to go. This way she'll merely go to sleep. When you think about it, wouldn't that be an act of love for the dog who has given you so much?"

I could feel a lump building in my throat and my head whirled. I had never considered killing Duchess. It never entered my mind. She was a friend, part of the family, part of my life. She was there in Grade School, Junior High, and High School, sharing our adventures. She was at the door to greet me when I came home on weekends while in the Marines. She was with me after the Marines, when I went to work and then entered college, and now suddenly I was asked to make the decision as to whether she should live or die. My knees went weak and small beads of sweat began to form on my brow. I pulled her close, even though I knew it must have hurt her and finally gave a slight nod of my head.

The vet stepped over to a cabinet, took out a syringe and a vial, held them to the light and pulled on the plunger. Back at the table, he found the spot he was looking for on her foreleg and injected the contents. Duchess nuzzled my chest, her rheumy eyes watching me and not the procedure. Almost immediately, while I held her, her eyes showed signs of glassing over and she began to sag and slipped from my grasp. There was no gasping, no spasms or convulsions; she just died quietly before my eyes, her body crumpled in a pile on the table. It was shocking. It was heartrending. I hadn't expected it to happen so fast. I hadn't wanted to watch her die, yet there she lay, a disheveled shadow of the vibrant and magnificent dog we ran with, played with and shared our lives with. I bolted from the room and out the door, tears streaming down my face, a wail of agony lodged in my throat. I had to pull to the side of the road three times before I got home, overwhelmed by grief and tears that I couldn't seem to stop.

I hated the veterinarian for a long time for putting me through that. How could he be so insensitive? Did he think I wanted to see my best friend die? How could he be so cruel? But, in the weeks that followed, I began to realize his concern was not for me but for Duchess. Duchess needed someone who loved her and whom she loved, to be holding her when she died. She deserved it and I had been wrong in my condemnation of him. Now there is comfort in knowing she left this world in the arms of one who belonged to her alone.

6
Fearsome Waters

I was stretched out on a float off La Jolla Shores, a beach resort north of San Diego. The sun beat down and a cool ocean breeze wafted across the water, creating the perfect atmosphere for dozing. In the hazy twilight of my musings I was remembering a documentary I'd seen a few evenings before on the sinking of the cruiser *Indianapolis* in World War II. The cruiser had just delivered the atomic bomb to the island of Tinian in the Marianas. It was a gruesome story in which a large number of crewmembers were eaten alive by sharks.

Rousing myself from these disturbing thoughts, I sat up, stretched and looked around. Time to go back, I thought, pushing myself to my feet. Looking to the shore, about the distance of a football field away, I could see children playing and people lying in the warm sun. The crystal clear water glittered in the afternoon glow and the sand, some eighteen feet below the surface, shimmered white and inviting when I stepped to the rim of the float. I had just launched myself off the edge and was still airborne when a large black shadow, menacing and sinister, shot out from under the raft. I only caught a quick glance at the ghostly shape but that was enough to send a jolt of fear through my entire body. Thrashing in the water after I surfaced, all I could think of was getting back to the safety of the raft. When I did reach the ladder, I scrambled up and flopped onto the deck, my pulse racing, my heart seeming to be permanently stuck in my throat. A few moments later I lifted my head and looked around. Nothing, no tell-tale triangular fin slicing through the sea, just placid blue water.

Lying there for some time, I attempted to calm my shaking body and decide what to do. I wondered, *should I try to call someone on shore to help me?* A second later I rejected the notion. With the roar of the surf and the screams of the children playing at the water's edge, it was doubtful anyone would hear me. I might try to get someone's attention by waving but there was only an off chance anyone would see me. I could stay where I was, and someone would call in to report me missing. Something in my psyche was holding me back from that plan. Perhaps it was the specter of being thought of as a wimp. More and more it looked as if I would have to extricate myself from this mess by getting in the water with whatever that thing was.

Finally, I screwed up all my courage, said a silent prayer, and slipped into the sea. Clinging to the ladder, ready to pull myself to safety in a hurry, I put my head under and took a good look around. Being somewhat reassured by seeing nothing, I began as quietly as I could to dogpaddle toward shore, constantly dipping my head under to scan the area below. Inch by inch I made my way toward safety but my progress was painfully slow. It was like a terrible nightmare I once had as a child. In my slow-motion dream, I was immersed in some sort of clear goo and trying desperately to run from something evil and unseen. The memory only reinforced my panic and I forced myself to concentrate on swimming and keeping a lookout.

When at last I felt close enough to shore to risk swimming, I struck out, still trying to be silent. I knew I was not yet out of danger, but with each second I was closer to the land and refuge. On the fifth or sixth stroke, when I raised my head for a breath, there, just inches away, a black shape rose to the surface. My heartrending scream was muffled by the cascade of water rushing into my wide-open mouth. Flailing wildly, my movements uncoordinated and clumsy, I thrashed blindly toward shore, all thoughts of silence lost in a mad panic to try to reach safety. At last, my hand touched bottom and I scrambled to my feet and staggered ashore. Dropping to my knees at the water's edge, my chest heaving and the world swimming in front of my eyes, I gave silent thanks for my deliverance. When I had sufficiently regained a bit of strength I stood on wobbly legs and looked out toward the raft, in time to see a black body torpedo out of the water up onto the float. My man-eating beast turned out to be a California sea lion, the 'clown prince' of the ocean. I must have been encroaching on his private sun deck. I didn't know whether I wanted to go out there and kiss him or kill him. It was an idle threat either way… I wasn't going back out there.

7
Experiments With a One-Way Submarine

On a gray and gloomy September morning in 1948, made doubly gloomy by the looming specter of school starting that following Monday, my brother Dave and I tried to lose our lives and almost succeeded. Two days before, we had spied a treasure amidst a pile of building rubble in a vacant lot three blocks from the house. (Although hard to believe now, at that time, there were still vacant lots in Pacific Beach, north of San Diego. Today you would be hard pressed to find such an animal.) The object of our attention was an abandoned tub for mixing cement and mortar. Approximately eight feet in length by four feet wide, it was shaped from two 2x12 boards tapered up at each end and fitted with a piece of sheet metal nailed to the bottom with roofing nails. At each end, 2x6 boards completed the box. The effect was a tub with a kind of Jon boat appearance. The sideboards were covered with dried plaster and split open in numerous places. A number of nail holes in both the boards and, for some obscure reason, in the sheet metal bottom bespoke rough treatment at someone's hands.

"Aw, Dave… I don't want to carry that thing home, its heavy." Actually, I wanted the would-be yacht and fully subscribed to my brother's plan but I was hoping he would carry it. It was the way of a twelve-year-old, at least this lazy twelve-year-old. Dave was unimpressed.

Of all our adventures, I cannot remember one where Dave was not in charge. He was older and besides, taking command of anything required energy and effort, commodities I reserved solely for daydreaming and the avoidance of work.

"Come on, pick up that end or I won't let you ride in it."

"Aw, jeez, can't we get a wagon or something?" I whined.

"Just pick it up or I'll tell Mom who broke the Robertson's gate."

"How did you know?"

"Butch told me."

"Oh," I groaned in defeat.

"Now, pick it up."

I doubt any beast of burden before me, or since, ever required so many rest stops to go three blocks.

"What, again? We just stopped a minute ago."

"Well, my arms are tired."

"Mom ought to take you to the doctor."

"Why?"

He didn't answer.

After depositing the prize behind Pop's tool shed I collapsed, exhausted, with my back against the wall.

Dave went rummaging. He brought out a can of black mastic roof tar and a stick. "Come on," he said, "let's seal it up." Using strokes Michelangelo would have admired, he began slapping the stuff in the holes. It looked like fun, so I joined in. When we had it all sealed, and tar spread all over the place, including ourselves, Dave asked, "What are we going to name it?"

I scratched my head, more out of puzzlement at the sudden democracy of the question than any effort to think up a fitting name.

"I know, we'll call it *Lurline II*," he announced. *Lurline* was the ship we came back on from Hawaii in 1941, after the Japanese attack. "Now we have to put in seats and make paddles." Neither of us thought of painting on the name, probably because we weren't sure of the spelling, but mostly we'd have to clean the brush or face Pop's wrath when he found it. With a plank across each end for a seat and two paddles made from cedar shingles nailed to broom sticks, we were ready to launch. Prudently we kept the plan secret from Mom for fear she'd crush the idea in its infancy. Somehow, she never seemed all that keen on our more risky adventures.

After tossing and turning our way into Sunday morning, we rose at first light, dressed in our new school clothes, including shoes and Mackinaw coats and then slipped out of the house. To this day, I'm unsure why we dressed in the new stuff. Perhaps it was to lend dignity to the proceedings, but I suspect it was more because we just wanted to wear them to see how we looked. It was still quite dark when we hoisted the boat and started for Mission Bay, two blocks away. Duchess, the third member of our team, was always up for any new adventure. She led the way, yapping and announcing our progress to one and all, awake or asleep.

Finally, just before I collapsed from aching muscles and exhaustion, we arrived at the water's edge. It was foggy and cold, but the tide was high. That was a plus because we could clear the sand bar that lurked twenty feet offshore. After launching our creation, we stood breathlessly watching it while Duchess looked from one of us to the other with questioning eyes. To our utter amazement and joy, it bobbed on the surface of the water like a cork. We were yachtsmen now, sailors with our own vessel. Stepping aboard and positioning our bodies in the exact middle, so she wouldn't lean too much, we struck out. Did we stay close to shore until we saw how it was going to ride? Not on your life. Did we take a moment to test the stability? No chance. Did we see if it would leak? Of course not. Instead we took off for the middle of the bay. By gum, we were deep-water sailors and there were oceans to explore.

Over the sand bar, offshore, we encountered our first difficulty -- the dampness we noticed in the bottom when we first boarded, was now half an inch deep. *Lurline II* leaked. It was only a minor problem because we could bail it out. That is, if we'd have thought to bring something to bail with. Not to worry, maybe it was just a little leak. We could always put our feet over some of the nail holes and slow it down. Then, just as we were about to go over the sand bar into really deep water, for some inexplicable reason, (still debated to this day), we decided we needed to switch ends. Both ends were exactly the same mind you, but each wanted to be in the other end for some unknown reason. Maybe it was to get a fresh prospective, or maybe it was to familiarize ourselves with every aspect of the boat's performance, who knows? We were trying to maneuver around each other when catastrophe struck. The water sloshing in the bottom amplified our movements and started the craft rocking. Each time she tilted, water poured over the side and of course, two experienced sailors such as we were, immediately shifted our weight to the other side and caused it to dip and overflow in that direction. Back and forth it went for a moment, sloshing water over the sides. Then she rocked herself gently to the bottom while the brave crew stood holding on to each other in frozen horror. Fortunately, she settled in four feet of water and we could stand up. Who knows what may have happened if we'd have been over our heads? Even though we were good swimmers, our heavy shoes, clothes and coats might have kept us on the bottom. Actually, it might have been better if we'd have gone down with the ship, because we now had to face the wrath of Nurse Russell.

Duchess pranced and yapped up and down the shore, excited by the new game, when two soggy, bedraggled and thoroughly chastened former seafarers slogged their way over the sand bar and through the muck and stingrays of the channel to dry land. Duchess by now seemed to sense something had gone wrong and had ceased the ruckus. The three of us trudged home in the gray morning to face the music. While we confessed to Mom what we did, she looked horrified and if she hadn't been so glad to see we were alive, I think she would have killed us.

School, Monday morning, saw the other students decked out in all their back-to-school finery. Not the Russell boys, we looked like a fashion replay from the year before. Our new togs were not yet washed and the coats and shoes we looked on so fondly would probably take a week to dry out. Neither of us could see it at the time, but at least we did come away from the adventure of our lives *with* our lives. Had we gotten out to the deep water, just the other side of that sand bar, while wearing those heavy coats and shoes, we might not have been so lucky. In the meantime, Nurse Russell was probably wondering what she'd created.

8
May the Best Liar Win

I'm kind of a used-to-be fisherman so I haven't drowned a worm in many a year. In my time as an angler, I admit a few times I may have told a tale where I embellished the truth just a wee bit. Through the decades though, I've found that all fishermen tend toward a touch of liberty with the facts, which gives a modicum of comfort to my own conscience. However, the worst lies I've ever heard were from that bunch of bass fishing liars in Phoenix, Arizona. Lordy, they could tell whoppers! Years ago, my next-door neighbor was one of them. He didn't fish. He was a little more aggressive than that. In his words he 'hunted' bass. After I got to know him, I found he too wasn't above a tall tale about the ones he'd caught.

One day we were talking over the fence and I was regaling him with a tale of one that got away. "Jim, this is no kidding," I said, "I was fishing on the Missouri River and I tagged into a catfish. Well, sir, I fought the brute up and down that river for an hour and a half when I finally lost him. I'd hooked him in the whisker and it tore loose. Mister, I don't know how big that fish was but that whisker weighed twenty-five pounds."

He didn't even bat an eye or crack a smile, which tells you the kind of devious mentality I was dealing with. "Heck," he said, "that ain't nothin'. Me and my son were night fishin' up on Roosevelt Lake a month or two ago and we had the Coleman lantern hanging on an oar out over the water. That dumb kid decided he was hungry, got stumbling around in the boat lookin' for a sandwich and kicked the oar. Of course, the lantern went right into the water. I was so mad I almost threw him in after it."

"What did you do?" I asked, picturing the chaotic scene in my mind.

"What could we do, but go home? The lamp was gone and we couldn't very well operate in the dark."

Boy, I thought, I'm getting a straight story here with no punch line. At last, maybe I'd found an honest bass fisherman… yeah, right. Then I found out he wasn't finished.

"Well, sir," he went on, "about a month later we were up on the same lake trolling and guess what we hooked into?"

"The lamp?" I asked, surprise and suspicion registering in my voice.

"Yeah," he said. Then his eyes got real shifty, his voice dropped and he said, "Now, if you'll cut down the size of that catfish, I'll turn off that lantern."

Can you believe it? It just goes to show you, the first liar doesn't stand a chance.

9
AS iF by Magic

Years ago, I was camped with a friend alongside a creek just outside Yosemite National Park in California. It was getting on toward evening and my buddy was down the creek somewhere trying his luck once more before the sun set. I'd just poured myself a cup of coffee and was sitting enjoying the quiet when a couple of strangers, obviously out for a walk, approached.

We smiled at each other. "Hi," I said and raised my cup in salute before taking a sip.

The man waved and said, "Hello, Bill."

I almost choked. *How in the heck does he know my name,* I wondered? My senses kicked into high gear and I thought, *do I know this guy? Where? Why can't I place him? Think, think! I must know him from somewhere, he called me by name. Maybe we worked together or he was from high school. He's going to think I'm an idiot if I don't recognize him.* I was verging on a panic attack.

As they were about to pass by, I screwed up my courage, swallowed my pride, and asked, "Do we know each other?"

They stopped and he said, "I don't think so."

I blurted out, "Well, how do you know my name?"

"It's painted on your coffee cup," he said, pointing.

I'm glad he told me; otherwise, I'd have been freaking out the rest of the night!

Speaking of spooky, let me carry you to another time and place. For awhile, when I was a kid, I thought a mysterious force had taken up residence in our refrigerator. I was convinced some sort of demon or powerful spirit lived there. It seemed like many times when I got in front of it, my head would go woozy and I'd get weak and dizzy. (Well, dizzier than normal for a pre-pubescent flibbertigibbet of nine.) The mystery remained unsolved and I'd probably have gone to my grave thinking our darned *Coldspot* was haunted. However, quite by accident, the solution came to me when I was about thirty-five and reading a prescription bottle. It said: *Warning, do not stand suddenly while taking this medication. This may cause dizziness and possible fainting.*

In a flash, I knew what was possessing me, and it wasn't a mystical spirit. I was jumping up off the couch and running into the kitchen. (At that time, I was jumping up and running everywhere and the food larders were my favorite destinations.) It was just coincidental that the time it took for the blood to drain from my head and render me goofy was about the same time I got in front of the refrigerator. In a way, knowing is kind of sad, because it was much more interesting and romantic thinking the ice box was haunted than accepting some sort of prosaic scientific explanation. Alas, another chunk of innocence lost and I don't think I'm any the better for it.

10
Mayhem on the Streets of Huron

DATELINE, HURON, SD. A local man was mugged while attempting to get out the back door of his house this morning, according to a police report. *Three thugs hit him on the head while others encircled him and one made for his pocket.* The investigating officer asked if the victim, Bill Russell, could give a description of the suspects.

"I dunno, it all happened so fast. Lemme see, they all must have been part of the same gang though."

"How do you know it was a gang?" asked the officer.

"Well, sir, they were all wearing the same getup. You know, gold with just a tinge of red. And, oh yeah, they all seemed to be about the same age, too."

"I know the bunch you're talking about. Seems every year we have trouble with them."

"Really? I'm from Southern California and we never had trouble like this."

"Yeah, well, here they run wild, clogging up streets and gutters. Seems like everywhere you look there's a bunch of 'em all going in circles and playing tag by the hour. This is the first time I've heard of them getting aggressive though. Most of the complaints I hear are about their being a nuisance and leaving a mess. You think you could pick any of them out of a lineup?"

"Maybe … although they all kind of look the same. I'll try."

"Let's start here at the scene. Maybe they're still hanging around. Check out that bunch there. Any of 'em catch your eye?"

"Boy, I dunno, all clustered up like that it's hard to tell."

"Here, let me separate them a bit…. How's that?"

"Well, none really stand out."

"I don't know, Mr. Russell, without a positive identification there's not much we can do."

"Yeah, I know, but I'd hate to put my finger on one and find out later he's innocent. I just don't see any of 'em. As I said, they all look the same."

"Well, one consolation is that in a couple of months, they'll all be in the slammer across the river. That's where most of these types typically wind up. The rest usually blow town and we never see them again." Then, he dropped his voice and kicked at a pebble on the driveway, "Problem is, next year they'll be a brand new bunch to put up with." He put his notebook away and turned to leave, but stopped. "You sure you're okay? You need to go to the hospital?"

"Nah, they didn't pack much of a punch and nothing got stolen, 'cept maybe my pride. What does this bunch call themselves, anyway?"

"Locals know them as leaves."

11

The Low-Down on Living It Up in Death Valley

For eight years, in the nineteen-nineties, I lived and worked in Death Valley, California, which is about as low as you can get. There is an organization called Death Valley Forty-Niners, or just 49ers for short. Every fall, they gather from all parts of the country for Death Valley Days and many take part in a trail ride from Ridgecrest to Furnace Creek Ranch, commemorating a famous rescue by two members of the trapped Bennett-Arcan party. The rescue itself had nothing to do with Ridgecrest but, due to several considerations, that was the chosen town for the start of the ride. Each year during the festivities, which include craft and curio stands, art displays, parades, dances, entertainment and cookouts, a lot of the people attend wearing costumes from that period. The whole thing is a big annual to-do in the valley.

To give you some history, Bennett-Arcan was originally part of a large group that arrived in Salt Lake City in October of 1849. They were too late to make it over the Sierra Nevada Mountains before the snow arrived. Two years before, the Donner party had been stranded in those mountains in what became a famous tale of survival. The place, Donner Pass, bears their name to this day. I won't go into the gory details but many in the party resorted to cannibalism just to keep from starving.

The Bennett-Arcan party was part of a group that split off from the main wagon train rather than wait in Salt Lake until spring. They followed a southern route known as The Old Spanish Trail, which skirts the mountains to the south, but adds about five hundred miles to the trip. Right off, their way was strewn with obstacles. There wasn't enough grazing for their animals, a deep canyon stood in their way and had to be crossed, water was scarce and there were no accurate maps available. The one map they had showed a range of mountains running east and west, some cartographer's pipe dream. Even though the map had inaccuracies, it was better than nothing. However, during the trip, the man with the map, who had joined the party in Salt Lake, took off and they were left with no directions at all.

Undaunted, the group continued toward the southwest in what must have been a slow and nightmarish trek. Eventually they entered Furnace Creek wash, which fed right out onto the floor of Death Valley and there, for the first time, they faced what looked like an impossible barrier. It was a near vertical wall called the Panamint Mountains, mistakenly identified by the group as the Sierra Nevada range. In reality, these hills were only pipsqueaks compared to that massive upheaval in the earth's crust farther west. Stymied and at the end of their tether, they sent two men bearing all the money they could collect and enough provisions for a couple of weeks to look for help. The pair walked out of the valley and all the way to a ranch near Cajon Pass, east of Los Angeles. There they purchased supplies, three horses and a one-eyed mule and then headed back. The horses didn't make it but fortunately the mule with the precious provisions did. It was a round trip of almost 300 miles, most of it on foot and an epic feat. With this in mind, let me tell you a little story connected with that event.

One afternoon, a couple of days before the valley began to fill up with visitors for the festivities, I was in the café at Furnace Creek Ranch. There were four gentlemen at a table, all rather on the slight side, getting along in years and decked out in western garb. A young girl, (I'm guessing she was new because I hadn't seen her at the resort before), was serving them. When she presented the check, her curiosity must have gotten the better of her and she asked, "Who are you and why are you dressed like that?"

"We're Forty-Niners," said a member of the group.

There was a moment of silence after which, with a perfectly straight face, the girl said, "Gee, you don't look like football players."

As the hooting and hollering died down, one of the other girls clued her in. Apparently, she had other things absorbing her attention when they taught that phase of our history at her school.

12
The Tragic
Consequences of Panic

In June of 1953, I was in my sixth week of Marine Corps boot camp when word came to me that I had lost two cousins in Death Valley, California. Neither was really a blood relation. Charles, the elder of the pair was twenty and the son, by a previous marriage, of my Uncle Charley. Skipper, just seven, was adopted. Nonetheless, it hit the family pretty hard and since I lived barely five miles from the base, I was granted a four-hour bereavement pass (unheard of in boot camp). It was two days later when the facts came out, but I didn't hear them for another week. This is the story that the authorities pieced together.

Charles took Skipper on a motor trip headed to Yosemite National Park, sightseeing during the day and camping out overnight. They were in their second day when they reached Lone Pine, California, gateway to Death Valley. Death Valley is brutally hot in the summertime, with temperatures often reaching almost 130 degrees during the day. The record for North America was 134 degrees air temperature reached at Furnace Creek Ranch, on the floor of the valley in 1934. Bad Water, 292 feet below sea level, is the lowest point on the North American continent. Ground temperature can go as high as 150 degrees in that area.

Charles talked to some of the locals in Lone Pine about going over there and they strongly advised against it. Apparently his motive, other than visiting the valley, was to add to his rock collection. Of course, at the time, Death Valley was a National Monument and collecting rocks would be a crime. Nonetheless, the next morning, against all advice to the contrary, he and Skipper set out for Bad Water. Temperatures in the valley were running about 124 degrees.

At the time, because there were virtually no tourists during the summer, the Park Rangers moved up on the Panamint mountain range to Wild Rose canyon. One ranger remained at Furnace Creek Ranch. That is apparently how Charles and Skipper managed to pass through the valley unnoticed.

A little beyond Furnace Creek Ranch, they turned south on the road that would take them to Bad Water, about seventeen miles down the valley. Before they reached Bad Water, however, there was a turnoff to Natural Bridge and they veered off onto the gravel road. Natural Bridge was uphill in a wash, a short distance from the valley floor. At some point, they must have tried to turn around and got stuck in the sand. There are a number of options to deal with this occurrence, such as jacking up the car and putting rocks or brush under the rear wheels, digging the sand out from behind the tires and even deflating the tires until they cover a wider area. Charles was a mechanic but apparently didn't know about these techniques or chose to ignore them. Having said that, I can imagine that in a panic situation one isn't thinking too clearly, especially when you feel like you're being roasted alive and you have a seven-year-old brother along. The next option would have been to take refuge in the shade of the car (not in the car) or the Natural Bridge and wait for evening. Vegetation is sparse in that area and trees are nonexistent.

Here is the tragic part. Charles (I say Charles because I think Skipper was too young to have a hand in the decision-making), decided they should leave the car and walk out. It was a fatal mistake. The nearest place they could go to was Furnace Creek Ranch and that was fourteen miles away. Also, they were trying to make the trip in the heat of the day. True, Death Valley does not cool down much at night, maybe five or ten degrees at most, but at least the sun isn't beating down on you, raising your body temperature. Then, to make things worse, at some point they took off their shirts and neither seemed to have a hat. After trekking back down the gravel trail, they reached the paved road and got a few hundred feet toward Furnace Creek Ranch before Charles must have collapsed. Skipper, some fifty feet behind, was apparently trying to crawl to him. They were found two days later by a Fort Irwin army patrol testing a hot weather vehicle. The bodies were in such terrible condition that the funeral had to be a closed casket affair.

I lived and worked in Death Valley for eight years and I know the dangers of travel there. Here in South Dakota, our biggest hazard comes from traveling in the winter. We can only hope we make better decisions in an emergency than did my cousin.

13

Societal Shenanigans

I sat down to write an article called *"The Acceptability of Old Attitudes Plaguing Casual Conversation in Today's Society"*. It is a deep and thoughtful subject, addressing the turmoil that is running through our nation lately. However, after showing it to a couple of people who looked at me like I was some sort of slime mold they found in their cornflakes, I decided to shorten the title to *"Political Correctness Run Amok"*. That was better anyway, crisp, but with no nonsense about it. Although the title seemed earthy and non-offensive, something was still bothering me. After agonizing over it for a couple of minutes, I realized I might be offending all the Amoks out there, even though I wasn't sure what Amoks were. It could be there was no such thing but I'd better not take a chance. It was safer that way.

Instead, maybe I can use the title, *"Political Correctness Gone Crazy"*. No, no, that won't do either. There are too many of them on the streets and they might take umbrage at the reference to their mental state. Of course, I could use, 'mentally challenged' in place of crazy but I don't think it has the same impact. Wait a minute, wait a minute ... aha, I have it, this is brilliant, and it won't offend anyone. How about calling the piece *"Politically Correct, Political Correctness"*. There, I don't think anyone can find fault with that title ... well, possibly my ninth grade English teacher or a logic freak somewhere.

I'm sorry – 'a purveyor of logical thought' is what I really meant to say.

It seems to me we're falling into a trap in this country. I don't advocate insulting anyone (especially if they're bigger than you are), but it's fast coming to a point where you can't hardly say or do anything without someone grousing at perceived discrimination or getting upset, imagining you're stomping around on the memory of their ancestors. The other day, I heard that people of the islands of the Pacific were riled up by the old tradition of wearing a couple of coconut shells and a grass skirt at college fraternity costume parties. It had something to do with stereotyping. Paaaleeease! What's next, Somali Pirates screaming about kids dressing up like Blackbeard for Halloween? So what if they do? Speaking of that, do you think the souls of our dearly departed will roar in outrage from their graves at a sheet-wearing seven year-old trick 'r treating in the guise of a ghost?

This has really gotten foolish. I am no doubt offending someone right now with this narrative. Guess what? I don't care. When I was in the Marines, sailors called us Jar Heads, Gyrenes, Leathernecks, and Sea-Going Bell Hops (among other things). Big deal, we referred to them as Swabbies and Swab-Jockeys. I once called a female Marine a BAM, which is slang for Broad Bottomed Marine (you figure it out). She was a Master Sergeant, big as the side of a house, with hash marks from here to there, and the disposition of a grizzly bear with hemorrhoids. (I never did that again.)

I don't advocate we intentionally hurt anyone, but I was never very good at walking on eggshells and I don't think I've gotten better at it. No, it wasn't good the way it was, but it's not good this way either. So, listen up you bunch of clowns in the SEI (social engineering industry), knock it off … I'm sorry, did I call you clowns… I meant to say Bozos.

14

Pearl Harbor I: A Surprise Visit

Seventy-three years ago, on December 7th, the United States was dragged into a war it had desperately tried to avoid for four years. On that morning, World War II started with a bang when the Japanese attacked the American fleet at Pearl Harbor. Germany, who'd been raging through Europe since 1938, threw in with Japan and we were in the fight of our lives. When the raid started, my brother Dave and I were playing in the back yard of our home in Navy housing across from Hickam Field Army Airbase and close to the harbor. At the sound of airplanes roaring over, we stopped digging in the dirt and stared up at the sky in fascination. There were always airplanes around, Army and Navy alike, but never this low. Our apartment, at the end of a four apartment unit, was right on the flyway to the Southeast Lock, a waterway that pointed like a bowling alley, straight at Ford Island and a mooring area known as Battleship Row. I remember the big reddish-orange balls on the sides and wings of the airplanes as they hurtled by on the way to their deadly mission. About that time, Mom heard the ruckus and came to the back door. After a quick look, she grabbed me and Dave, dragged us in the house and stuffed us in the closet under the stairs.

"Stay in there until I tell you to come out," she yelled and then she slammed the door and we could hear her pounding up the stairs screaming for our father. This story was fashioned from accounts told over and over during the time I was growing up. This is the way Pop used to tell it to gathered friends and family over the years:

"Claudia came bursting into the bedroom yelling at me, 'Get up, Al, we're being attacked!'

"Huh? W...what are you talking about? I mumbled. There were some loud roars coming through the windows. I rolled over, pulling the pillow over my head.

"'We're being attacked by the Japs,' she yelled, poking me and pulling at the covers. Just then, almost like it was backing up her words, a plane roared by and shook the house.

"'Oh, that's just maneuvers Claudia; they buzz the fleet all the time.' While I was saying it, I heard a faint series of booms in the distance.

"'Al, it's the damn Japs. Get up, they're bombing Pearl Harbor!

"'Claudia, it's just Army maneuvers, nothing to worry about.

"'Get out of that bed, Al, we're at war!' The crashes and booms outside were getting louder but I still wasn't worried. I rolled out and headed toward the bathroom.

"'Where are you going?' Her words were almost drowned out by the sounds of another airplane.

"I'm going to get a shower and then take the boys down to see the show.

"'The hell you are, Al Russell!' When she started talking like that, I thought I'd better go to the window to have a look."

Mom liked to jump in at this point of the story, *"By then I think it was beginning to dawn on him that these might be something other than maneuvers."*

Pop would roll his eyes, make a face, and then continue:

"When I looked out the window and saw all the smoke, I wondered, 'why are they burning off sugar cane fields on Sunday morning?' The, a strange airplane flew over, right above the house-tops and I saw the reddish-orange rising sun on the side and a big torpedo hanging under its belly. I thought, 'I don't remember any Navy squadrons with that insignia. It must be the Army.' Just then, another loud booming sound came through the walls.

"'Here, put these on,' Claudia said handing me my pants."

Mom usually took up the story from there:

"He looked at me and turned back to the window, his mouth hanging open. One more glance and he yelled, 'I gotta go!' It was as if he were just waking up to the idea that something was wrong. Still struggling to button up his pants, he went out the door with his shirt tail and shoelaces flapping."

Dave and I never did get down to see the 'big show' — maybe it's just as well. We spent the next two hours shut up in the closet. There, we whiled away the time brandishing a couple of homemade weenie roasters (short sticks used as handles with a piece of coat hanger wire nailed to them), and vowed they weren't going to get us. We took an oath we were going to fight to the death. Neither one of us knew what death was other than what cowboys did in the movies, but we weren't about to become victims of the Japanese. We really didn't know what a Japanese was either and it's a wonder we didn't poke each other's eyes out with those weenie roasters.

15
Pearl Harbor II:
In The Afterglow

An hour or so after the raid ended, Mom let us out of the closet. Along with neighbor ladies and their children, we stood in the back yard watching the smoke roiling up from the harbor and scanned the sky for airplanes. A few seconds later, I glanced down and spied a jagged piece of metal under my tricycle. To this day, I haven't figured out if it was a piece of a Japanese bomb, or one of our own anti-aircraft shells. I suspect it was the latter. It has been a prize possession of mine all these years. One of my uncles just had to get in on the glory too — he cut one end off with a hacksaw because he wanted a souvenir for himself. I never liked the sleazy bum after that.

During the bombing, Mom and the neighbor women erected a fort in the kitchen where they hid. It consisted of mattresses on top of and around the table. It was a marvelous place and we kids took over, gleefully wriggling in and out of the dark confines playing Cowboys and Indians while waiting for lunch.

I think it was during a family get-together after the war that Pop described his arrival at the submarine base headquarters building on that terrible morning:

"I could see all the smoke and hear the explosions in the harbor while I hoofed it up the road toward the base. At the end of Southeast Lock, I could see Battle Ship Row. The

Arizona must have just blown; it was a loud 'wooosh' and a pressure wave, rather than an explosion. Oklahoma was rolling over, and any lingering thought that this was maneuvers seemed to evaporate. There was shooting somewhere behind me, so I stepped it up a notch and when bullets slammed into a building next to me, I put it into high gear and got the heck out of there."

"Weren't you afraid?" one of Mom's sisters asked.

"I was too scared to be afraid."

"Oh," she said, as if that were a perfectly logical response to her question. She was kind of ding-y anyway. I guess that's why she was a favorite of mine.

When the tittering and guffaws stopped, Pop went on:

"I ran into the main building at the base and saw a bunch of officers standing at a window in the hall, watching while the fleet was being demolished. I don't think I've ever seen such long faces. After milling around for a while, I decided I couldn't do anything there, so I went down and got a cup of coffee."

Dave and I have mulled over this conversation numerous times through the years. In one of our discussions he said to me, "Jeez, you really think Pop did that?"

"I guess. You know Dad. He does everything different."

"You realize we may be the only kids in the world with a father whose first act of war was to get a cup of coffee?"

If you knew our father, you'd understand how that could happen.

Night crept over the island and with it new fears could be seen in the faces of the adults. People were on edge, waiting for the next calamity. Rumors were rife, anything from poison in the drinking water to a Jap invasion fleet sitting off Waikiki Beach. One of the women heard that the local Japanese were rising up and killing everyone they could find. Another heard Jap paratroopers were landing on the Pali in the Ko'o'lau Mountains. That story was interesting because islanders had long told tall tales about people jumping off the Pali and then having the wind blow them right back up. It begged the question — why would anyone with a parachute want to land there?

That evening, shortly after the house got dark, my sister Fran went to the refrigerator and opened the door. The light came on and she was practically mobbed by people diving to shut it off.

"Put that light out! Don't you know there's a black-out?"

"How can I get in the refrigerator?"

"You can't."

Hunger, the real mother of invention, triumphed and Fran covered herself and the refrigerator with a blanket and opened the door. Later, some smart person unplugged it, unscrewed the light bulb and plugged the box back in.

After a while, two neighbor ladies stepped out onto the front porch to get fresh air. Their cigarettes drew the attention of a couple of roving sentries from Hickam Field who suggested they put them out or get shot. Prudently, they dowsed the butts and stepped back inside. It was a very jittery time.

Dave and I slept fine in the mattress fort, but I think Mom and the neighbors spent a restless night huddled by the radio. Of course, it wasn't broadcasting because the local government was afraid the Japanese could home in on the transmission and find the island. It didn't occur to anyone that the Japanese had already found the island and knew exactly where it was and if they didn't, the fires still raging at Pearl Harbor were a dead give-away.

Pop was stationed aboard the submarine *Plunger* (SS 179) when he brought the family to Hawaii. In 1940, he transferred to the mine-laying submarine, *Argonaut* (SS 166). *Plunger* survived World War II and was stricken from naval records in 1957. *Argonaut* was sunk on her third war patrol in 1943 by Japanese destroyers with the loss of all hands. Pop had already transferred off the *Argonaut* so we were spared that heartache.

16

Pearl Harbor III:
Time to Skedaddle

The day following the attack, in order to get civilians away from the military installations, we were evacuated back to Honolulu and moved in with our former landlord on Lahala Lane. It was an exciting time and three days before we saw Pop again.

"David, Billy, boys, it's time for bed."

"Neat, do we get to sleep there?" we squealed in delight, pointing at the mattress on the floor.

"Won't that be fun?" Mom asked as she kissed our foreheads.

We wriggled under the sheet and watched in surprise while she flopped another mattress on top of us. "Aw, Mom, do we have to sleep under that?"

"I want you to because this way you'll be all snug and safe."

It may have been all snug and safe but as I remember, it was darned uncomfortable too.

Next day, Mom took on a strange chore for someone living in the islands; she went looking for coats, sweaters and warm clothing. The stores didn't carry such things because there wasn't much call for them. We dutifully followed her to the Salvation Army, Goodwill and any thrift shop she could find. The problem was, she was in competition with everyone else going back to the mainland.

December in San Francisco is a lot different from the same month in Hawaii and people who had spent much time in the islands had either outgrown or gotten rid of their winter clothing. It was a rag-tag bunch that headed back to the States dressed mostly in ill-fitting and mismatched outfits.

We boarded the Matson steamship *Lurline* on Christmas Day. The reason for the delay? The ship was two days out of Hawaii on her regular run to San Francisco when the attack happened and she got an urgent call to turn around and pick up civilians being evacuated from the island. By the time she loaded, made the round trip, reloaded and was ready to sail, it was nineteen days later. Mom, Fran, Dave and I shared a stateroom with a young navy wife and her baby. They crammed as many in a cabin as it would hold.

Most of the facts concerning the voyage I learned over the years by listening to conversations between adults. However, at least one of the mysteries I solved myself, quite by accident. The first afternoon on the ship, standing in line to enter the dining room, we were next to a wall of red, yellow and blue polka dots. I didn't discover what the wall was made of until a year or so later when I was in a grocery store with Mom where they sold Wonder bread. On board the ship they had to find storage for the overflow of foodstuffs needed because of the excess number of passengers so they put racks of bread in the hallway. Had it not been for a trip to the store, I might have gone through life never knowing what all those colored dots were about.

I don't know which one made the other one ill, but Dave and Fran got seasick on that first night, and took to their bunks. The smell in the cabin was horrendous and when they were asleep, Mom took me outside and we sat on deck chairs where I promptly fell asleep. Apparently she did too but woke up a couple of hours later. For years I told the story that we sat outside the whole night but that I think was an error. However, it did make the tale more dramatic that way and I came out looking like the hero.

The loudspeaker blared at supper on the second night, "No passengers will be allowed out on deck tonight." As one, the crowd jumped to their feet, color draining from many of the faces and eyes darting about, unsure what the message foretold, and whether they should be alarmed. It showed the level of anxiety present on the ship. After all, we were in the middle of the ocean, on a ship packed with people, just days after the Japanese attack. Safety and security didn't seem all that sure anymore.

Mom, telling the story to friends said, *"I guess people had a right to be uneasy. There was only one destroyer escorting us so most of us felt like sitting ducks. After seeing what they did to our fleet, it was hard not to."*

On the bright side, however, one other night, in slightly rough weather, there was a show in the auditorium. I don't recall what it was, maybe a movie. I do remember we were sitting on blankets on a highly polished hardwood floor and every time the ship tilted, people slid downhill and then back when it pitched up the other way. It was wonderful, if you were a kid, but now I wonder if the adults enjoyed it as much – no, probably not.

My sixth birthday fell on our last day at sea. I'm certain there was a little celebration of sorts but I don't remember it. I do recall the ride was wild that day and almost made me sick. The ship stopped off the entrance to the Golden Gate to wait for a harbor pilot to take us in. The swells were huge, probably from some storm at sea, and the ship lifted up on each crest and plummeted down into the next trough some thirty to forty feet below. It was like a roller coaster and made my stomach feel funny. Apparently it made other people's stomach feel funny too because they were lined up at the rail. It sounded like they were all calling for someone named "Ralph."

That afternoon we docked at the terminal in San Francisco, safe in the bosom of the United States once more. The war years were just starting and 1942 was to be a mostly black year for the country. But Dave and I were kids and it was an exciting time to be alive.

17

PEARL HARBOR IV — Easy Money iF you Have the Stomach For it

After World War II, my father's favorite 'gotcha' story centered on Mona, a German shepherd dog we had in Hawaii. Pop was stationed in Pearl Harbor on a submarine and we lived in Navy housing across from Hickam Field, near the harbor. When the Japanese attacked on December 7th, the dog, spooked by the explosions and noise, took off and we didn't see her again until some months later. The family, except Pop, sailed back to the mainland on Christmas Day. A few months later, the Humane Society contacted us and said they'd found her cowering in the sugar cane fields and were shipping her to us. It was a tearfully joyous reunion. From here, let me tell the story as Pop would have when he had his victim cornered:

"At that time, Hawaii was not yet a state and the American money had HAWAII printed in black letters across the backs or the bills. This was so the money stayed in the islands. When they evacuated the family, Claudia smuggled a small roll of bills back to the states as souvenirs. One day, she had the money out showing it to a friend when Mona got hold of it, and swallowed the whole roll. Claudia tried everything she could think of to get the

dog to upchuck the money but nothing worked. Finally, not knowing what else to do, she called the veterinarian for advice. He told her to pour croton oil down the dog's throat and lock it in the garage. He assured her that even though it would be messy, she should retrieve the bills. The kids helped her hold the dog and pour the stuff down its throat. It was no easy task, the dog wasn't thirsty, but finally the bottle was empty and she put poor Mona in the garage. Four or five times each day for a week, armed only with a set of tongs, she checked out the dog's progress."

At this point the listener, usually very attentive and concerned, would ask, "Did she ever find it?"

The hook was set and Pop would reply, *"No, she never did. You see, the money was Hawaiian and the dog had a hard time passing it in the U.S."*

Through the years, that line must have produced thousands of sniggers and groans but the family stopped listening after the first twenty tellings. By then it had lost its luster to everyone but Pop, and those who hadn't heard it yet. I confess that I still like to tell it.

18

The War Years I: Into the Jaws of the Unknown

Reminiscence Department: The next six articles showcase the trials and tribulations for Billy Russell while growing up during the war years in San Diego.

Following the December 7th attack on Pearl Harbor, my mother, sister, brother and I moved from Navy housing near the submarine base back into Honolulu. Then, on Christmas Day we boarded the Matson passenger liner *Lurline* and headed for San Francisco, passing under the Golden Gate Bridge on the final day of 1941. At the dock, we were met by Mom's sister and her husband, who lived in Alameda, across the Bay. It is interesting that my only real memory of our stay there was visiting a lumberyard where my uncle worked. Dave and I had our picture taken on a stack of lumber. I probably remember it because I still have the picture.

There was one other incident I recall, probably only because the story was told over and over though the years as I was growing up. It happened on the stairs of the apartment where we stayed. One morning we were going someplace, I can't remember where, but Dave and I were trooping down the stairs ahead of the others. The women were chattering merrily one step behind when something was said to pique Dave's interest. He looked up with his mouth wide open just as mom flipped a long ash off of her cigarette. Guess where that wad of ashes went? Dave finally recovered his breath amid backslapping and whooping gales of laughter from the spectators. My uncle always added at the end of the story, *"The lesson was simple, stay out from under Claudia's cigarette or keep your mouth shut."*

Here's the thing about being a kid: I'd have gladly swallowed the whole darned cigarette if I could have been the hero of the story. Even then I was kind of a ham. He got all kinds of recognition from that tale and I got none. Life is so unfair.

Three days later, we headed south toward San Diego. I don't know whose car we took, probably my aunt and uncle's, and I only remember smatterings of the trip down the coast. I do recall it was gray and cold. In the late afternoon on a mid-January day, we rolled up in front of a pretty white house, set on top of a hill in Ocean Beach, overlooking the Pacific Ocean and the California shoreline stretching to the north. It was a glorious view and one that would captivate me for the next four years. This, the house of another aunt and uncle, was where we were to live until Pop came home after the war. After the initial hug fest, chattering gaiety and hoopla, Dave and I were led to a hall closet absolutely overflowing with gifts. It was a paper-tearing orgy made all the more spectacular because Christmas was over. The staggering array of toys and clothes piled on the floor boggled my mind. I liked it, I mean I *really* liked it. Such a Christmas was the thing kids dream about and usually only the rich ones get to experience. It turned out it was the last display of Christmas opulence until after the war.

We kids were never privy to the worry and concerns of the older people during those first weeks of the war. Most adults were very anxious, and afraid the west coast was the next target for the Japanese. My brother Dave, Johnny Johnson (a buddy from across the street), and I had our own priorities. There were vacant lots to explore, alleys to wander and trashcans (yielding an occasional treasure) to be picked through. All this and not enough hours in a single day to accomplish these delicious tasks! We were blissfully ignorant of the savage struggles going on in the Pacific and across the Atlantic in Europe. Of course, we knew the slogans: *Kill the Japs, A Slip of the Lip Can Sink a Ship* and *Remember Pearl Harbor*. Later we learned the words to *God Bless America*, sung by Kate Smith on the radio, over and over and over. I was happy when *Rosy the Riveter* came along, it was a change. Early 1942 was before food and gas rationing began so the peanut butter and jelly flowed freely and there was plenty of milk to wash it down.

However, there was a dark hole in the fabric of life that no amount of peanut butter could gloss over. Favorite nightly radio shows like *The Shadow* and *Red Rider* were given over to news broadcasts. It was all so unfair. Couldn't they do that some other time? Maybe during the day when soap operas like *One Man's Family* were playing would have been better. At least, I thought so. My soul thirsted for *Red Rider* and his adventures, not all that other stuff. On Saturday mornings we religiously listened to the fairy tales performed on *Let's Pretend*. Even though it wasn't all bad, it was still a trying time of cultural deprivation for a kid.

It was in that same year that I launched my brilliant academic career. Barely two years later, that career crashed in flames when I was held back for another go at the third grade. The sting of such a trauma haunted my dreams for many years. My memories of the time are not all that fresh and in fact only exist in quick and fleeting flashes like scenes from one of today's wild music videos. It is no doubt the result of that childhood trauma that the next eleven years were such a scholastic flop. Well, I gotta blame it on somethin'.

19

The War Years II: Class, This is Billy Russell

My first day in school, I remember a mammoth teacher in a flowery dress escorting me to class, and a sea of strange faces all staring at me like I was some sort of alien life form.

"Class, this is Billy Russell. Say hello, Billy." I mumbled something unintelligible while studying the floor with great interest. "You may sit right there, next to Sharon Frost."

I remember the staring was still going full blast when I took my seat and tried to make myself smaller. Later, for lunch, I sampled the delights of a dry bologna sandwich and tepid milk from a less than efficient thermos. However, all these hardships were forgotten when, during the lunch hour, I saw boys playing with their toy boats in the dirt under a row of trees along the fence. I knew right then what I wanted to be the rest of my life: captain of a ship made out of an empty ice cream cup filled with dirt in which a piece of paper, impaled on a stick, was stuck to represent a mast and sail. The fact that the hull was round didn't seem to bother any of these sailors and I jumped right into the middle of it. I found a cup in the trash along with a piece of paper, scrounged up a twig and soon I had as smart a craft as ever sailed the stormy dirt of Ocean Beach Elementary school.

Over the next months, recess and boats were my only interest and all that other school stuff I considered a waste of time. I did like the stories the teacher read aloud while we sat in a semi-circle on the floor around her chair. She particularly seemed to favor the *Wizard of Oz* book, although there was a smattering of other classics: *The Little Engine That Could* and one other story, I believe it was called, *Mike Mulligan and his Steam Shovel*. It was all about a guy and his mechanical shovel which wound up being the heater for a building when they couldn't get him out of the hole he dug for the basement. There were endless Dick and Jane tales to buck up our moral fiber and instill a sense of fair play. It was during these sessions I learned such catchy phrases as "Run, Jane run," and "Jump, Spot jump." All in all it was great stuff.

Actually, life was pretty cushy then and I'd probably have been content to move through the seasons of my existence and into my dotage playing boats, eating peanut butter sandwiches and listening to stories but alas, nature intervened. There is some sort of passage in the book of life that says one must grow and move on. It all seems so unfair somehow. I mean, here I'd carved out the perfect existence for myself, a life of ease and adventure. To be evicted just because I'd stayed too long was almost criminal. Nonetheless, toy boats gave way to finger painting, daydreaming on a higher-consciousness level and modeling clay.

The clay caper started innocently enough. I was simply going to borrow some of the supply to practice my sculpting technique at home. Now, all you would-be clay snatchers, pay heed to my warning: never put a wad of clay in your pocket on top of your handkerchief – it could be your undoing too. In the reading circle I sniffled. You know the drill, stuff running down your upper lip that you keep sucking back in instead of expelling.

"Billy, don't you have a handkerchief?"

I nodded yes but when I reached for it, a wad of goo blocked the way. Oh my gosh, I'd put the clay on top of my handkerchief and it was all stuck inside my pocket. I was undone. I panicked. Even if I could remove the warm, sticky mess from of my pocket and free the handkerchief, everyone would see it. All would know there was a hardened criminal among them. I could see myself rotting in jail and my short life passed before my eyes. Jumping to my feet I rushed back to the clay table digging at the sticky mess in my pocket, hoping I could get it out before the teacher, who was now on the prowl, arrived to see the immensity of my transgression. But she swooped down on me before I could get rid of the evidence. I was caught like a rat in a trap.

"Billy Russell, were you trying to steal that clay?"

I stood frozen, unable to speak, for there in my hand was the evidence. With nose stuff running down my lip and horror in my heart, I automatically shook my head 'no'. She loomed over me like an avenging angel, her face contorted in a sneer and she snarled, "Come with me young man."

In a line-up of one, I was made to stand in front of the class and listen to the terrible words of the indictment: "Class, what do we think of a boy who would steal clay?"

I never found out what they thought. No one spoke, although a couple of 'goodie-goodies' groaned. I was busy studying my shoelaces which, of course, were untied.

There was a terrible silence, an awful void in the fabric of the universe where my tormented soul wallowed in the muck of disgrace and guilt. Then those merciful words, "Sit down Billy," signaled the end of my public torment; however the private horror still lives in my breast, even to this day. It marked me for years and made me unable to perform even the most rudimentary of shady tasks such as sneaking into the loge seats when I only paid for a general admission ticket. Even before it got started, my criminal career was cut short, nipped in the bud as it were, never to achieve its full potential. I was doomed to a life of obedience to the rules – well, sort of.

I rejoined the semicircle a crushed man, beaten down and exposed. Immediately I began planning what I was going to tell my mother should the need arise. I wanted desperately to blend back in, to become just another face in the crowd. It was somewhat of a challenge with gunk running down my lip and once again I was singled out for special attention. "Billy, use your handkerchief."

"Yes, Ma'am."

20
THe War Years III:
GiRLS, YucK!

The war brought a lot of changes and one I remember vividly. Each morning before school, all the students and teachers gathered in the courtyard for the flag-raising ceremony. It was a solemn occasion and at the time, the thing was tightly choreographed to show maximum respect for the colors. At eight o'clock the flag went up the pole. Everyone put their hand over their heart. Some of the younger ones weren't too sure where the heart was and consequently the hand was free to roam just about anywhere. The teachers made a valiant effort to correct as many as possible before the ceremony started. When all hands were located someplace acceptable, we started: *"I pledge allegiance..."* At this point we were to extend our hands toward the flag, palms up and continue, *"To the flag..."* It was a nice touch and was very respectful except certain of the nasty little boys (not to mention any names) did it palms down in the Nazi salute they saw in the newsreels. It wasn't long before the extended arm was dropped, so to speak, in favor of just holding the hand over the heart... or, wherever you thought that spot was. As far as I know, the palm up version was never readopted... anywhere.

After school it became a ritual to run across the street to the library and feed the fish in the large pond out front.

The woman at the desk gave us wafer squares that looked like pressed bread or a cracker. On more than one occasion, the fish went hungry when we ate their food ourselves. What the heck, it was an adventure in flavor and, as kids, we were naturally always hungry. Eventually, the lady behind the counter got wise and informed us that the fish had already eaten. It seems that girls were a much more reliable distributors and the fish thrived after they took up the chore. It was a definite blow to our masculine pride and empty bellies. On the bright side, who knows what was in that stuff – we might have sprouted gills if we had kept it up.

I was, and still am, in awe of girls. I didn't understand them then and that perception has not improved over the years. It was like they were from some other place. They liked to stay clean and read books. They wouldn't try such delights as getting down and wallowing in the dirt or eating fish food. They were perplexing to me and it seems no amount of time is going to improve my understanding. Oh, I don't mean all of them were so different. There were a few that liked to get down and dirty but I thought of these few more as one of the guys than girls.

Sylvia Brassy was a prime example of the first type, not the second. I think she ran home at least three or four times a day to get her dress ironed. As a boy, rumpled was my normal condition, a sort of devil-may-care look. My sister Fran preferred the word tacky. She was one of those clean freaks too and being only my sister, I ignored her opinion. Older than me and bossy, she was always ordering me and my brother around. One of the most galling tasks I remember doing was dishes. While she got to wash them,

Dave and I had to dry and put them away. She was always done before we were which proved to me her job was easier. Complaining to Mom didn't do any good and I suspected it was because she was a girl too. Consequently, I went to her with my scrapes, cuts and bruises, but never with questions concerning sexual equality.

Getting back to Sylvia, her hair was always perfectly combed, and her face and hands washed. She had a clean fresh smell about her and her shoes were shined. Sitting next to her during reading sessions, I felt like a weed in a patch of daisies. Worse, she ignored me as if I didn't exist, even though I tried every trick in the book to get her to notice me. (The book of tricks for a six year old is pretty thin.) I was head over heels in love with a goddess and she didn't even know I was alive. More than once I trudged home a defeated man. Unrequited love will do that to you. My only solace at the end of the day was a couple of cookies, a glass of milk and *Jack Armstrong, All American Boy* on the radio.

Eventually, Sylvia's place in my heart was taken over by Marilyn Coats. She at least looked at me and once she even smiled. I wandered with my head in the clouds for two days. Don't read anything into this, that's where my head usually was anyway. Even then my heart was fickle and since then I've had thousands and thousands of 'loves'. They seem to come and go like skin cells. Lose one and it's immediately replaced by another. Most girls, of course, weren't aware of my feelings and went blithely about their business while I secretly pined away in misery. Life can be cruel to those who love. It didn't occur to me that other boys might have the same dilemma. We never talked about girls at that age, unless they were one of the guys and ate fish food.

21

The War Years IV:
A Talent For Dawdling

Early in my career as a child, I learned the art of dawdling. It just seemed to come naturally to me. I can't say it has been helpful in the same way that learning to put a little English on a marble or telling which plums were ripe in a neighbor's tree when it was totally dark outside. It did teach me to relax and gave me an appreciation for what turtles go through in their daily meanderings. I became so adept at slow motion that my mother claimed there were times she found it difficult to tell the difference between my conscious state and a full-blown stupor.

There were certain advantages and responsibilities that came with this 'gift'. First, it had to be used judiciously; it didn't work for every occasion. For instance, when it was time to wash the dishes, an urgent trip to the bathroom was a much more effective work reducer, even though my brother screamed to high heaven about it. Once in awhile this backfired and I came out to find my share of the work still undone. In the main though it came off pretty well. Yard chores presented a special brand of problems that the bathroom ploy wouldn't cure. This usually called for some heavy duty loafing. The object was to look like I was working, but only *look* like it. Eventually Mom would tire of standing over me and take up some other task. On one record day I pulled exactly two weeds! It was one of my more memorable performances, but who could I brag to? (That was in the days before the Guinness Book of Records started keeping track of such wondrous accomplishments.)

However, laurels aside, dilly-dallying was almost my undoing on more than one occasion. One time I remember particularly because it was my first brush with the law. I had slipped into the practice of dawdling on my way home from school. There were numerous vacant lots, a sure-fire attraction to an adventurous youth such as myself, and more and more I stopped to indulge in exploration and play. True, I was catching flack at home for the practice but not enough to really deter me.

"Billy, where have you been? You should have been home a half hour ago."

"I stopped to look at something, Mom."

"You come home first, and then you can go out and play. Do you understand me, young man?"

"Yes ma'am."

The next day, however a new pile of trash at one of my favorite stops arrested my attention. Drawn like a magnet, the lure was irresistible. Half an hour later I sauntered into the house, ready for a cookie and milk, and even though I was waiting for the usual tirade, nothing was said. That should have set off warning alarms in my head but I just figured Mom was weakening and that maybe I was free at last to explore the world at will – to come and go as I pleased. Somehow the cookie tasted extra good that day. I was savoring my victory and a second cookie when a loud knock came at the front door. I followed in the wake of my mother, curious to see who was knocking so vigorously.

When she opened the door, there stood the biggest policeman I have ever seen in my life. He filled the doorway and blocked out the sun. I peeked out from the safety of Mom's skirt.

"Is he home yet?"

"He just got here."

"Is that him?" he asked, pointing a massive finger at me.

Mom stepped aside and I was exposed, finked out by my own mother. With knees shaking and heart in my throat I stood paralyzed, unable to move. The half-eaten cookie in my hand was forgotten as I faced this behemoth alone. Funny, before then I had never considered myself to be small. Now I felt infinitesimal.

"Step out here Billy." The voice was deep and menacing.

I moved closer to the safety of Mom's skirt but she pushed me away and toward the door. The awful truth struck me in a blinding flash. She was in cahoots with the giant in blue. My head reeled and I felt faint standing there in his shadow.

"I hear you stopped to play again on your way home from school," he said in a booming voice. His words hammered me and I wondered where he had heard that, then in another flash of insight I knew.

I looked down at his gigantic shoes and stood mute. I couldn't muster enough spit to wet my mouth or enough breath to answer.

"Did you?"

I nodded my head 'yes' but remained silent. Somehow crying, my first line of defense in these situations, seemed inadequate.

"I'm going to be watching you, young man, and if I catch you not coming straight home and checking with your mother after school, I'll have to arrest you and put you in jail."

I wasn't sure what arrest meant but it didn't sound pleasant. Still I was unable to speak. My knees were rubbery and threatened to give out on me at any moment and my chin quivered in a prelude to the tears.

"I don't think you'll have any more trouble with him, Mrs. Russell. If you do, please call me." With that he saluted, turned and walked out to his car. In the house Mom never said a word. She didn't have to, I was a changed man – I'd seen the light.

22

The War Years V:
I Have to Eat What?

During the war, it seemed everyone had a 'victory garden' in their back yard. Not only was it practical because of the food shortages but also patriotic. Bugs probably got a lot of the produce and, with a few exceptions, this seven-year-old would have been content to let them have it all. If it wasn't a potato or carrot, I wasn't interested. I remember not being able to eat potatoes for a month after I saw one with a worm in it. Even though Mom assured me she'd cut out the bad part and the rest was perfectly good, I just couldn't convince my mouth to go there. The fact that he'd been living in that same potato was enough for me. It so unnerved me that, to this day, I won't eat potato chips with dark spots on them.

Our garden sat in the back corner of the lot, tended daily by mom, my sister Fran, my aunt and grandmother. They'd all been raised on a farm in Arkansas so the thing went pretty well. When they could round me up, I was forced to pitch in once in a while but only when I couldn't get away. My view was – it was slavery of the cruelest kind couched in the guise of family participation. Usually Mom found it was far less trouble to do it herself than be on me for every chore and most times I got to skip. It was the only advantage to being the youngest that I ever discovered. I vowed I was never going to live on a farm no matter how many stories I heard about 'the good old days'. In retrospect, Dave seemed to have a green-tinted thumb and even appeared to enjoy grubbing in the good earth. I was always suspicious that he was sucking up. Consequently, I watched very closely to make sure I got my fair share of everything. It disturbed me to see he was getting in so solid with the bosses.

Later, he branched out on his own. There was a narrow strip of land between the garage and a sidewalk. He decided to move on to bigger and better things and plant a cash crop. He carefully dug up the strip and planted flower seeds of some sort. I didn't know what kind since my interest in the project was just on the far side of nil. Each morning he would water them before school and each afternoon when he got home, he would dig them up to see if they were growing yet. Eventually he gave up the project after determining the seeds were probably no good.

Vegetables have never been big with me, and spinach was not even in the same universe. Even though *Popeye* seemed to love the stuff, just one look at his arms and, worse, *Olive Oyle,* convinced me that *Spinacia oleracea* wasn't good for you. I could handle green beans, tomatoes, carrots, potatoes and corn but that was just about the limit. One day, instead of the usual bologna or peanut butter and jelly sandwiches, Mom gave me money to eat in the cafeteria. It was novel and I looked forward to the experience. She carefully tied the fifteen cents in the corner of my handkerchief and sent me on my way. I don't remember what the entrée was but in one of the compartments of my tray they slopped a spoon full of cooked squash and tomatoes. Carefully, I ate everything on the tray but that. I had managed to avoid even touching it, fearing some sort of personal contamination. When I made my way to the trashcan to dump the stuff a teacher was standing on guard. Before I could get rid of the disgusting slop she stopped me and said, "Why haven't you eaten your squash?"

"I don't like it," I confessed.

"Do you know how many children are starving in India who would love to have that food? You go back and eat it. I'll be watching you, sit right there."

That old argument never worked for Pop and he was my father. I sat down and looked at the gruesome mess. Ten minutes later, I was still looking at it when the cafeteria was just about empty. She approached. "You haven't taken a bite of that. You're going to sit here and finish every bit of it. Now get eating." She sat down across from me and said, "I'm going to watch you so get to eating, it's good for you."

It was a death sentence, the ultimate nightmare, an impossible task. Even if I managed to get some in a close proximity to my face, my mouth would refuse to cooperate. I already knew that.

"Eat," she snarled. "You're not leaving here until you've eaten everything on that tray. Now get to it."

I just looked down at the slimy mess and sat there.

"Okay," she said, reaching over and picking up the fork. "I'm going to feed you just like you were a little baby." She scooped up a fork full and shoved it under my nose. "Open up."

I did and she wore the contents of my stomach the rest of the afternoon.

"How was your lunch Billy?" Mom asked when I got home.

"Oh, fine," I lied. "Can I have another cookie? I'm still hungry."

23

THe War Years VI:
Would You Hold the LT
on that BLT Please?

At a very young age I must have been attacked by a vicious vegetable of some kind and established the root of my aversion to the species. I don't mind living in the same neighborhood with the leafy beasts, I just don't want to be too chummy. I've always maintained a workable relationship with broccoli, turnips, rutabagas and the like; they keep their distance and I keep mine. These facts alone make the following story a bit hard to swallow, if you get my drift.

By the time I was in the fourth grade I was already in awe of a rich kid named Steven Snooty. I knew he was rich because he got to ride to and from school in a big car, bring his lunches in a real metal lunch box, not a paper bag, and his clothes didn't have gobs of patches like the clothes I and most of the other boys wore.

Sitting across from him at lunch one day, I was feeling especially shabby because I was in my oldest garb. It was laundry day and my good set was in the wash. I watched agog as Steve held up a culinary masterpiece. Alabaster slices of white bread piled high with crisp bacon, lettuce, thick slabs of rosy-red tomato and oozing with mayonnaise.

After gawking at that scrumptious-looking work of art, I glanced down at the dry bologna sandwich in my hand and experienced a life changing revelation: vegetables notwithstanding, I must have such a prize for my own! Nothing else would do. I would never again settle for less. Envy was pouring out of my ears and I was going to make my feelings known that very night.

At dinner I broached the subject. "Mom, can I have a sandwich made with bacon in my lunch tomorrow?" Her eyes grew wide. "And, oh yeah, can you put some lettuce and tomato on it?"

Her jaw dropped just like in the cartoons. "I . . . I was going to give you peanut butter and jelly the way you like it."

"Oh, Mom, can't I have bacon, lettuce and tomato, puleeeeease?"

"Billy, you've never wanted anything but peanut butter or bologna before. How come now all of a sudden you want a BLT?"

"No, Mom, I want a bacon, lettuce and tomato sandwich, not that thing you spelled. What is it anyway?"

"That's what BLT means, bacon, lettuce and tomato."

"Oh."

"Billy, I can't even get you to try lettuce. How come you now want it in your lunch?"

"I saw Steve Snooty eating one today and it looked so good. Can I have one, please?"

"Okay, but you're going to have to eat it if I make it for you. You sure you want it?"

"Yes'm."

I could hardly sleep that night in anticipation of the morrow. Boy, was I going to show Steven Snooty that my mother cared too. I was going to whip out that culinary triumph and dazzle him. Next morning, the Wheaties and milk tasted extra good and I had a second bowl while Mom prepared my mid-day feast. I skipped all the way to school, there to settle in and wait for lunch. The hours ticked by slowly and my mouth watered – I could hardly wait for lunchtime. I don't know why I'd never eaten a BLT before. While waiting, I thought, maybe I can slip the lettuce off and hide it while no one was looking. I might even try some, maybe just a little — no, I don't want to go too far the first time out. I'll just play like I'm eating it.

Finally the big and little hands were lined up on twelve and the bell rang. My moment was at hand and, shaking with anticipation, I proudly carried my lunch sack to the table, making sure I sat close to Steven. Then, with a flourish, I reached in the bag and took hold of my prize. My jaw dropped as I viewed the catastrophe. I was stunned, caught off guard because in my trembling hand was a soggy, gooey, red mess of glop. The lettuce was wilted and limp, as was the bacon and the bread was mush. What had happened? Why was his so perfect and mine such a disaster? I pushed it back in the sack before anyone could see it and left the table mortified. It took years before I finally figured out what happened. Apparently what I missed was, he took the lettuce from one wax bag, the tomato from another, the bread from — well, you get the idea.

After school, Mom asked me how I liked my sandwich.

"It was good," I mumbled.

"Maybe I'll make you another next week." I lived in fear she'd do just that.

"Can I have something to eat?"

"Are you still hungry?"

"Uh huh."

24

Why, We'll Stop That Leak in Just a Jiffy

In high school, my auto mechanickin' savvy, on a scale of one to ten, was somewhere down around a minus three. However, compared to my brother's talents in that department, I was a genius. Even though he was eighteen months my senior, his abilities were only slightly above that of an amoeba. Between the two of us, our MIQ (Mechanical Intelligence Quotient) romped in at a whopping zilch, that is to say zero. Keep these facts in mind so you can properly appreciate the following story.

Sometime around 1951, coming home from high school and a few blocks from our house, Dave and I found a 1939 Chevrolet 2-door sedan for sale and we just had to own it. We pooled our resources, with the idea of purchasing it but had to concede that $18.43 was far short of the $200 necessary to complete the deal, so we approached the folks. After an intense period of pleading, begging, groveling and a solemn promise to pay it back, we got the $181.57 we needed to close the deal, a king's ransom at the time. Flush with the cash, we turned it over to the seller and the Chevy was ours. Dave drove it home while I sat proudly in the passenger's seat holding the precious paper and checking out every minute detail of the upholstery and interior. He had his license and I only had a learner's permit at the time. That was alright, I was content to ride and it was glorious tooling around the neighborhood in our very own car. We showed it to everyone.

One of the not-so-hidden features of the car was the automatic oil change. It leaked oil and so in a couple of weeks all the oil in the crankcase was brand new, saving us that chore. Of course, everywhere we parked, people knew we had been there. It was a constant battle to find a new spot so we didn't leave too big a mess. Our driveway was dirt and that made it safe to park it there.

Dave, who was the oldest, which made him the captain, decided one Saturday morning to fix the leak. Remember when I told you earlier about our thorough lack of experience in anything mechanical? We, who didn't know one end of a wrench from the other, were about to tackle a major auto repair. This was the stuff they used to dredge up to make *Laurel and Hardy* movies.

The oil was coming out of the bottom of the engine so of course we started at the top, taking off this and looking under that and wondering what this thing did. All very entertaining and educational but not much help when it came to putting the stuff back. Just remembering where it went, let alone what went with it, was a major issue. We finally worked our way to the underside of the car and Dave took off what we found out later was the clutch dust cover pan. It had a hole in the bottom and we, being old hands by now, decided it shouldn't be there. After all, that was where the oil seemed to be leaking. The remedy? Put one of the leftover bolts from up top and a nut Dave scrounged up somewhere in it and plug the thing up. Perfect, we'd stopped the leak. There were still a few screws and nuts left over but she seemed to run okay so we filed them away in a box, took her for a test spin and congratulated each other on our accomplishment.

Two days later, on our way home from school, the old buggy began to slow down. The engine was running good, but the car didn't seem to want to move anymore. By the side of the road we noticed our oil leak was back, only this time it was spilling over the top of the cover we'd 'modified'. With sweat flowing freely, and muscles complaining because they were unaccustomed to such toil, we pushed, pulled, and cussed the Chevy the last three blocks to the house. Befuddled over this new development, we were at a loss to figure out how it happened or what was causing the malfunction. One of our uncles shed light on the problems at a family get- together the next night.

"You gotta leave that hole open so any oil leaking out of the rear of the engine can drain away. Right now, the pan is probably full and the clutch soaked in oil."

"What do we do?"

"You're going to have to replace the clutch plate."

"How much will that cost?"

"Around ten bucks, I imagine. That is, if you boys do the work."

Together we groaned, "Oh."

He must have caught the depression in our voices because he said, "There is one thing you might try first." When he laid out the plan, it was like a giant weight being lifted off our shoulders.

The next morning, we pulled the plug out of the bottom of the pan and drained the oil, pushed the car across the street and put the front bumper up against a big tree, started the engine and let it sit running in gear for awhile until the clutch began to grab a little bit. The old car never quite got up to speed after that, but at least it ran and it beat the heck out of walking.

About two months later I got lazy and didn't check the oil before I took off. It was empty. I burned the engine up and it seized. Again we were walking and I wasn't too popular in my brother's eyes. Worse, we had only made two payments of $20 bucks each and we still owed $141.57 on a car that wouldn't run. It was a very depressing time of life.

25

Gas Guzzlin' Brother

The gas gage in the old Chevy didn't work. It hadn't worked from the day we bought it and to combat the possibility of running out of gas, it was our practice to put a quarter's worth in the tank when we were going somewhere. Bear in mind, that was back in the days when the fuel-flow dial on the gas pump ran faster than the dollar dial. That phenomenon has not been seen in a long while and most young drivers today never saw it at all.

If it was a bunch of guys out for a lark, we pooled our money and that determined how far we were going that trip. On occasion, when Dave or I had a hot date, we'd put in fifty cents or maybe a dollar's worth, but those were special occasions and you sure as heck didn't want to leave any gas for the other guy. Such is how brotherly love works. Dave and I had committed most destinations to memory. For instance, my girlfriend lived on the end of Mission Beach, a distance of one point eight miles. Round trip was approximately three point six miles. We had calculated the old car got about fifteen miles to the gallon, which was just a guess really. I don't remember how we arrived at that figure. Therefore, I reasoned one gallon of gas would transport me to my love's house and back four times … that is unless Dave got hold of the car and used it up between my trips of l'amour. To combat this possibility, I drove it to the outer limits of the calculated gas range and brought it home almost dry. I know, I know, this sounds crass and mean-spirited but I was in a war. He was doing the same thing to me.

And so it went, a battle of wills, each guarding his turf and hoarding his supply of 'go juice', fearing the other brother might use some of it. Weeks went by where we shared the car, but never the gas. Then one night, I was taking my girl to the sophomore prom. She was a year behind me and Dave didn't have a date. This was going to be a big night and I pulled into the station and ordered the attendant to put in a dollar's worth. A few moments later he came back to my window and told me the car wouldn't take it, it was full. The thing would only take thirty cents worth. I was stupefied. All this time we'd been putting gas in and leaving little bits and it finally filled the tank.

Of course, the honorable thing to do was to tell Dave so he could share in the bounty. That would be the right course of action. I know he would do that for me … it was only fair – after all, we were brothers. Hey, wait a minute, wasn't he the guy who stole my baby bottle and drank the entire contents in front of me while I screamed in rage and helpless behind the bars of my crib? (I don't remember the incident, but Mom used to tell people the story to my shame and embarrassment). And, now that I think about it, wasn't he the one who ratted me and Butch out the day we cleaned Mr. Evans plum tree of all the fruit? As I remember, Mr. Evans got his revenge because I spent the whole day in the bathroom.)

I put the car in gear and let out the clutch, smiling. *I'll pick up Jeanine and after the dance, take a nice long drive, maybe up the coast to Oceanside to a drive-in for a hamburger.* Gad, it was fun being rich.

Some days later, coming home from Jeanine's, the old car quit running. I knew there was gas in it, I'd checked the miles, and there should have been plenty. It had to be something else. Suspicion fell on the fuel pump. I pushed the lifeless hulk to the side of the road and 'hoofed' it home.

Next day I scrounged up eight dollars, bought a rebuilt fuel pump, took it to the car and installed it. Voila, back in business. I cranked the engine over, then over and then over again. Nothing happened. I took the fuel line off and tried it again but no gas came. I was beginning to get a sinking feeling. You remember my batting average with mechanical problems in the last story? It was zilch. It turns out I miscalculated and the car was out of gas. Twenty-five cents could have solved the problem and saved me a lot of hassle. Oh, well, at least we now had a spare fuel pump. That was something.

26

A Honeymoon For Three

In 2010, Norelle Bartel and I met here in Huron, courted briefly and decided we liked each other. I had to return home to Southern California and we emailed for a few months, discovering we really were kindred spirits. She flew in to San Diego to visit and meet my family, and we took a little side trip to Yuma, Arizona for a weekend. It was on Fourth Avenue, the main drag of that hamlet, that I pulled up to a yellow light, proposed while it was red and got my answer before it turned green. (I didn't want to give her time to think about it.) What a glorious day – we couldn't wait to tell friends and family! To my chagrin, my daughters seemed perfectly willing to let me come back to South Dakota but wanted Norelle to stay there with them. Now I ask you, does that seem fair? I finally extricated her from their clutches and we traveled to Salt Lake City to spend Easter and visit her daughter there. Once again, I was free to go but they wanted her to stay. Humiliation aside, it only confirmed what I already knew, I had me a winner. After another hug fest, my intended and I headed east to start our new life. In May of 2011, we pulled into Huron and the sweet insanity began. Meeting family and friends, making plans, sending out invitations and eating … lots of eating. I was operating under a tremendous handicap inasmuch as I do not remember names or faces. To conceal this character flaw, I just smile and nod my head a lot. It works until I'm asked a specific question, and then I'm sunk.

My first inkling that Norelle might be as whacky as I am came when she suggested we have Clyde, my pet tin chicken, shipped out here to be our ring bearer. (He was featured in the *Plainsman* article, "A Fine Feathered Friend", dated May 24th.) I was agog and delighted. I knew right then this thing was going to work to perfection, and that I'd found someone with a matching silly gene. Nothing could mar the gaiety of the moment. Even Norelle's impending trip, five days after our wedding, was a non-issue. She and her good buddy, Janice, had booked and paid for it months before I ever came into the picture. That's okay, I'm pretty good at puttering around alone as long as there's plenty of peanut butter.

We married on the front porch of a son's house in Yale on a beautiful sunny Saturday (the next day the yard was flooded by a torrential downpour.). It's as I suspected, this woman has an in with He Who Has Sway Over Everything. She even managed to get us a nice day for the wedding. I think I better stick with her.

A week later, she and Janice boarded a bus for their tour. When they got back, she told me about the looks they received when they told everyone that they were on our honeymoon trip. It really raised eyebrows. That wouldn't have worked in California ... those people would have just thought it was normal. Maybe that's one of the big reasons I'm here in South Dakota.

27

Do Opposites Really Attract?

I honestly don't know if they do or not. Through the decades, I've lived believing this premise simply because someone, I think it was my grandma Casey, said it was so years ago. For some inexplicable reason, the other day this subject came up in the Russell household. I got one of those questions every husband knows is out there and is going to eventually come at him like a rocket: "Honey, why did you marry me? I mean, we're so different." This is dangerous turf and the male of the species had better be prepared for it in advance. I was literally saved by the bell. The phone rang, giving me a half-hour or so to ponder and reflect. I find, at my age, I'm doing a lot of pondering and reflecting.

When Norelle and I met, I was living in San Diego, she in Huron. I had seldom lived anywhere but Southern California and the southwestern deserts. I was a gypsy. Having dropped my bedroll in so many places, I'd need a calculator to keep tabs. She, on the other hand, was a seventy-three year resident in the same town and thirty-five of that span in the same house even. It's amazing! I think I once lived in the same place five years… no, make that almost five, a record in my case. Alas, Mother Nature tossed a couple of extra days at me in the form of leap years and so, even though I lived there a solid five years (5 x 365, or 1825 days), I really lived there two days short of that mark (leap years have 366 days). Never mind, it's a trifling point.

Getting back to our differences, Norelle loves to eat vegetables, even such exotic and loathsome specimens as green peppers and squash. My relationship with roots, tubers, leaves and such was to keep a respectful distance. It's not that I have anything against vegetable eaters; it's just that I preferred to be a bystander and watch from afar. I got all the vegetative nourishment I needed from French fries, catsup and an occasional lettuce salad.

Well, that changed. Since we married, I've been railroaded into consuming vast quantities of things they dig out of the ground, whack off the top of things that grow out of the ground and wrench from very suspicious looking bushes. Thank God for peanut butter, bread and a busy wife who, of necessity, leaves me to my own devices periodically.

Norelle makes the bed daily, cleans the house, and washes the dishes, all very commendable. In Billy Russell's world, such chores would have always been put off until they reached critical mass. Now I live in the world of the clean and efficient. Pleasant, but nonetheless foreign. I'm not saying I was a slob, just a bit tacky and unmotivated. I have gone for days with the bed unmade. What the heck, I was just going to mess it up that night anyway and that pile of laundry in the corner would sit quietly if unmolested. With clutter and sloth, I tried to maintain a non-confrontational relationship.

In my childhood, my idea of charitable giving was sharing with my dog, Duchess, the occasional meal of liver forced on me by Mom. That dog knew the strategic places to be, and on liver night that was under the table. I admit, there were times I did feel a teensy-weensy bit guilty about the praise heaped on me for my clean plate … although never enough to 'fess up'. In 1953 when I joined the Marines, the first lesson I learned was 'never volunteer for anything', and I never did. That has kept me in good stead with my lazy side all these years.

Now Norelle has me going to church and volunteering all over the place. Of course, my puny efforts in that department don't even come close to the full court press that woman puts on. It's infectious. I don't mean it makes me volunteer more but it wears me to a frazzle watching her. Former friends and associates of mine would sit dumbfounded and agog at the Bill Russell they would see before them today. In truth, they would be no more dumbfounded or agog than I.

Do opposites attract? I don't know, I hadn't thought about it for years until she brought it up. They must, how else could we have gotten together? P. S. I really love and admire my dear wife and revel in our differences despite the funny food she thinks is so good for me.

28

Horticultural Horror I: I Was So Sure They Were Melons

It has been said that insanity is doing the same thing over and over and expecting a different result. If that's true then I must be nuts. Before I get into that, let me give you a little background. I was raised in San Diego, lived most of my working life on the deserts of the southwest, and probably would have remained there if I hadn't met and married a wonderful South Dakota woman, Norelle, and moved to Huron.

That out of the way, I can recount for you the first time I ever tried to plant anything. It was watermelon seeds in 1948. Technically I didn't really plant them. I was eating watermelon in that particular spot in the backyard and a few days later, up they came. I guess if you really want to be generous, I did sort of plant them.

At the age of twelve I was experiencing the pride many a father must feel when they see their children for the first time. I convinced myself I was enthralled with the burgeoning life forces spreading before me and each morning before school I'd check them out. Of course, this was all bunk. My sole interest in germination and the agrarian process was so I could gorge on watermelon all summer.

Fortunately, I didn't follow my brother's example in his first horticultural foray. A few years before, he had planted a row of flower seeds and although he carefully watered and tended his patch, he also came home from school each day with his curiosity inflamed, and dug them up to see if they were growing yet. You can guess how well that went. I was spared that temptation because these were already sprouting when I noticed them.

Time went on and my vines crept outward, gaining strength, and then one glorious day I discovered tiny blossoms. I was ready to pass out cigars and notify the newspapers. A few days after that, tiny balls appeared where the flowers had been. There was no denying it, I was going to feast on watermelon – my own watermelon – probably the finest ever grown anywhere. As I watched, they grew and soon they were the size of my favorite aggie shooter marble. Beautiful pale green little orbs that someday would grow up to slaver the interior of my mouth with heavenly delights.

If only fate hadn't thrown me a curve ball. By brother and I were told we would be visiting Texas to see my grandmother and uncle. None of my protestations secured a stay and in the end I had to leave my little melons for awhile.

Before leaving I entered into an agreement with my best buddy, Butch, from across the street to tend the melon field in my absence. In return he was to share in the bounty. A quarter of those plump, luscious beauties were to be his. Off I went to Texas, confident my fields were safe. A week later, off went Butch to the Colorado River with his folks for an extended vacation.

Three weeks after that, I boarded a bus for the return trip to San Diego. All I could think of was my melon patch with those blob-shaped juice factories ripening in the sun. When I rounded the corner of the house, I pulled up short and my heart fell. There were the same puny little green golf balls I'd left the month before, clinging to their shriveled up vines and hard as walnuts. I doubt you could even crack one of the darn things. As far as I know, they're probably gracing a roadbed somewhere with all their other rocky brethren. Thus ended my first attempt at horticultural dabbling, which turned out to be a disaster.

Next week, I'll tell you the tale of a planting job that succeeded beyond my wildest dreams – I'm still trying to live it down.

29

Horticultural Horror II: A Bloomin' Nightmare

In 1964, I lived in a townhouse in Phoenix, Arizona. At the time I was working twenty-five miles to the west and commuted across the desert daily. Our backyard was about the size of a postage stamp and surrounded by a six-foot, grape stake fence. I decided to beautify the area with a flower garden. The last time I practiced any sort of horticultural activity was in 1948, which produced the great watermelon disaster. However, I was confident I'd learned a lot since then. (I don't know why, I hadn't tried planting anything.)

I dug up a four-foot square patch, and removed all the grass. Next, I put a brick border around the plot, mulched and fertilized the soil and, when everything was perfect, I planted a packet of assorted flower seeds. The picture on the front of the packet set my heart ablaze. I just knew that was how mine would look. The sweat flowed freely and even cramped muscles failed to dampen my inner pride at my accomplishment.

Each day after work I watered and inspected my little plot. My joy was boundless when at the end of a week a tiny leaf popped up right in the middle. As the days passed, more and more sprouted and I knew the pure joy of having created something good. Faithfully I watered and tended my plot and everything grew so nicely that I was thinking perhaps I'd missed my true calling. Maybe I was destined to be a farmer.

One little plant seemed to grow better than the rest and after a few days, I fancied I had a good shot at a blue ribbon in the county fair. I kept watering and feeding and tending. It grew and grew. Soon it towered over all the rest. They, in turn looked puny and stilted. My horticultural masterpiece kept growing and spreading, getting bigger and bigger all the time. What looked like tiny yellow flowers adorning its delicate branches that seemed about to burst into full glory egged me on. I watered and tended and my enthusiasm was undiminished, even when all the rest of the tiny sprouts had shriveled and died out.

By now, my prize was almost to the top of the fence and spreading out to cover half the back yard. I heaped more water on it and redoubled my TLC (Tender Loving Care). The flowers were just on the verge of opening. I spent hours admiring my creation and plucking trash and stray leaves from its lovely branches. It just had to be my magic touch that produced such a glorious specimen.

There comes a time when, even the densest among us, must begin to hobnob with reality. I must admit that a tiny black cloud of suspicion had taken root in the back of my mind. Just a gnawing feeling something wasn't quite right. However, I was too deep into flora parenthood to back out now. I continued the watering and feeding and soon my flower stood two feet above the back fence. Then, my world of pride and self-congratulation came crashing down on me.

One afternoon, while riding home from work with the carpool, there was a lull in the usually boisterous conversation and I happened to look out at a desert wash. My heart stopped and I gasped and cringed, agog at what I saw. There, before my disbelieving eyes, were acres of these things!

The awful truth dawned on me, I had been feeding, watering and nurturing a weed! My shame was complete, my sin exposed and I'd be laughed out of the community. Friends and neighbors alike would talk of me and nod with knowing smiles. To make my humiliation even more painful, I had to buy an ax just to cut the darned thing down. By then the trunk looked like something standing in the redwood forest and the root ball left a gaping crater like a World War II *Blockbuster* bomb. Any lingering thoughts of a career in horticulture were dashed on that terrible day, so long ago.

In the next episode I'll tell you about taste buds driven to the edge of endurance by anticipation, and left broken and torn on the dust pile of desire. Sounds like a tag for a B-rated movie.

30

Horticultural Horror III: Inversion as a Method to Limit the Size of Tomatoes

I'm a tomato junkie. Be it in salads, on sandwiches or just sliced and topped with mayonnaise, set me next to a nice ripe tomato and I'm one happy dude. That's why, when the advertisement for that upside-down hanging tomato planter played on television, I sat enthralled. The sight of those plump, juicy red beauties hanging like a cluster of grapes set my mouth watering. I knew I just had to have one of those gadgets. Never mind my dismal record of agricultural failures dating back to my childhood, this looked like a perfect setup. At least, that's how it was presented in the advertisement.

When my wife found one of the contraptions at a local store, I was ecstatic. I couldn't wait to get home to begin the process that would load my table down with rosy-red delights. Thoughtful to the end, she also purchased a tomato plant of the beefsteak variety and I was on my way to horticultural history. I had the Guinness Book of World Records squared in my sights.

When we got home, I carefully assembled the bag and hung it on a wire hook dangling in front of my window. The hook originally held a small bird feeder. This would be the perfect place. Plenty of sunshine and I'd be able to watch my beauties grow. Placing the plant in the bag presented a bit of a challenge requiring both me and my wife to accomplish. The plant must have been around the store for awhile and had grown much bigger than the hole where it was supposed to go. With adroit manipulation and some serious pulling and tugging, we managed to snake it through while only losing half the leaves and a couple of branches. Then came the crucial task: filling the bag with soil. This takes a deft hand and a gentle touch. It also helps if you don't mind getting a little dirty.

Each layer had to be evenly distributed to fill the bag and avoid air pockets. If there was one problem, one bump in the road to success, it was the wire hanger. It was soft, easily bent and with each scoop of soil, the bag got heavier and heavier. Soon the wire could no longer support the weight and the hook began to straighten out under the load. I managed to catch the bag just before it would have crashed to the ground and crushed the fledgling plant beneath. It was obvious a much sturdier anchor was needed. The steel shepherd's pole promised opportunity but it practically bent double when I tried it there. What was required was something sturdy, something like a 2 x 4 screwed to the side of the garage. A half-hour later I was in business. Now I could begin the tender loving care that would guarantee weeks of dining pleasure.

I watered it daily and fed it according to instructions on the box and, after what seemed to me like an eternity, blooms appeared and then three tiny globs. I was ecstatic. Of course, I was expecting dozens and I thought they should have been the size of baseballs by then. But not to worry, I was confident the rest were waiting in the wings, ready to pop out at regular intervals to grace my table with a continuous supply of goodies.

Weeks passed and my daily inspections revealed a disturbing trend. Even my untrained eye could see that the growth was a wee bit slow... heck, it was almost nonexistent. The other thing was that the leaves looked funny, they were curled up. I thought it might be from heat but they stayed curly even when it was cool which scotched that idea.

Still I waited. According to my calculations, by now there should be scads of big, ripe beefsteak tomatoes, hanging like Christmas tree ornaments. Instead, I had three little green marbles that could pass as 'jaw breakers'. What really hurt was, not only did I never experience the joy of eating my own produce, but these hardened little steel balls cost me about nine dollars apiece to grow. I can buy a lot of tomatoes at the farmer's market for that kind of money and I bet they taste just as good as if I'd grown them myself … maybe better.

Epilogue: The three marble tomatoes have gone missing. I suspect the squirrels got 'em. My humiliation is now complete. I'm seventy-eight and with any luck the next time a planting frenzy comes over me I'll be gone. That in itself will be some sort of relief.

31
Fogeydom, Codgerdom or Geezerdom?

When you're a kid, you don't think much about the years. You're not five or six, you're five-and-a-half or almost six (never just a little past five). A friend once explained it this way: when you're five, one year represents one-fifth of your total experience. However, when you're fifty, one year represents only one-fiftieth of that experience and therefore has a smaller value.

During your teens, the years just can't seem to go by fast enough. I suspect *Playboy* magazine had a lot to do with that mind set. You're in such a rush to grow up, everything else is secondary… except maybe food. After you reach young adulthood, you're so busy learning to drink and debauch, you don't worry that much about the time. There's always plenty of it. Later on, work, home chores, fussin' with the little woman and the kid's need for braces occupy most of your waking hours.

However, when the end starts creepin' up, you begin to reevaluate your priorities and take stock of what is important. For instance, those high-calorie desserts you avoided all these years suddenly don't seem so threatening. Remember, you used to tell yourself you'd rather kiss a tarantula than lay a lip over grandma's yummy fudge and caramel drizzled cake with cherries jubilee ice-cream, smothered in a half pound of whipped cream topping …. (I think I just made myself hungry.) Now, suddenly close to the other end of the spectrum, you start wishing time would slow down, or even stand still. The only time it seems to do that is while waiting for that social security check to come in. That sets us up for a discussion about the three stages of our dotage. Can you guess what they are? Here's a clue, they end in 'd-o-m'.

Stage 1, Fogey-dom. In the main, *Fogies* still function pretty well. As a group, they normally take pride in their dress and appearance, although sometimes forget to zip up. Having lived through the turbulent nineteen sixties and seventies, they never miss a chance to show off the leisure suit they say they bought in Haight-Ashbury. (More likely it was the Penney's store down the street.) That toothpaste dribble adorning the front of their best double knit shirt, if they even saw it chances are they'd think it was just part of a tie-dye design.

Stage 2, Geezer-dom. *Geezers* are oftentimes seen with mismatched socks, wearing shirts with more wrinkles than an elephant's armpit and their trousers inside-out and backwards. They usually spend a huge amount of time wondering why their pockets are now next to their skin and can't imagine how their suspenders got so turned around. The clue usually comes when they reach for their wallet and discover they forgot to zip up. Geezers are still functional, however, they are very unpredictable and extremely high-maintenance.

Stage 3, Codger-dom. The *Codger* is a different animal. He no longer sweats trivial things but focuses on the big picture. With him, boorishness is a badge of honor and he wears grumpiness like a suit of armor. He's concerned with such vexing questions as: *Did someone really see LBJ carrying a rifle on the grassy knoll that morning in Dallas*? and *Was the Hindenburg trying to light up in a no-smoking zone?* Questions not reported in the daily news but explored in depth on talk radio. He dotes on reruns of the *Lawrence Welk Show* and shots of the Champagne Lady dancing on Larry's accordion. Ask any *Codger* and they'll tell you they don't bow down to anyone. I tell you, *Codger-dom* is so empowering and liberating it …

"What's that, Honey?"… "I thought I did take out the trash." … "Really?"…"Look, can I do it later? I'm right in the middle of this article and…. Well, yeah, I did say I would and I'll do it… Oh, alright." You know, it's unnerving when your wife is a bigger *codger* that you are. "Okay, okay, I'm going…. Geez."

Oh, did I mention, *Codgers* tend to be very impatient too? By the way, I have one daughter who swears I went from *Fogey-dom* to *Codger-dom* without ever passing through *Geezer-dom* …. "Yeah, yeah, Sweetie, I'm going…." I can't get away with nothin' anymore.

32

Even Apes Have Chewing Limitations

I attended my first auction when I was in my fifties. Up until then, I'd led a sheltered life, away from the rough and tumble of the bidding wars. At the time, we were living in a rented trailer on a pig farm located outside Lancaster, California and owned by a widow lady. Two other tenants lived in a cage in the front and across the lawn from our porch. I don't know what kind of apes they were but they stood about four feet tall and looked like they'd be more comfortable mugging drunks in an alley somewhere than swinging from a tree. The other feature that pushed the mugging theory along was some serious dental hardware that looked like they could chew their way through Hoover Dam. I mean, these babes had some major league choppers.

At the time, we had a bid in on two-and-one-half acres and I was beginning to fancy myself a gentleman farmer. I don't know why, the closest I'd been to a farm before this was to drive past one along the highway or when I watched *Green Acres* on TV. So, here I was on a Saturday morning, hobnobbing with other *agrarianites*, looking at shovels, clippers and a myriad of other farm implements, most of which I knew nothing about. I did notice that the majority seemed in pitiful shape and I found myself idly wondering if that increased their value.

Later, carrying a 'new' hoe with a taped-together handle and a rake with six or eight tines missing, I found myself standing with the crowd in front of a wall of little cages filled with mostly chickens, ducks and rabbits. In this go-round, I should have remained just a spectator. I had no facilities to start my vast herds yet (*do birds gather in herds?*) About half-way through, the auctioneer pointed to a cage with three white chickens and asked if anyone would give fifty cents for these fine birds. No one spoke. I thought, *Boy, fifty cents for a chicken dinner, wow!* Cautiously, I raised my hand.

Immediately a guy in the crowd shouted, "Fifty-five!"

My reaction was swift and authoritative: "Sixty!" I said, a bit of angst rising in me. I thought that would shut that clown up.

He fired back with, "Sixty-five!"

I couldn't let him get away with my birds for that price! In my mind they were already *mine,* dangerous thinking at an auction. I shouted, "Seventy-five!" I was certain that should take care of that Bozo. It did, I was suddenly the proud owner of a trio of fifty-cent chickens I'd paid half again as much for.

The idea I was up against a shill, a phony bidder whose job it was to drive the price up, never occurred to me, at least not until later when I thought about it. I was too busy planning a magnificent Sunday supper of *'Russell Fried Chicken'* with all the fixin's. At that time, I was also dabbling in fantasies about culinary triumphs. I don't know why. About the only accomplishment I had in the kitchen was a fairly tasty peanut butter sandwich (if I got the right bread).

I took my prizes home and set them loose in the yard to fatten up for the feast next day. My mouth was watering so much that I could hardly wait. In the morning, totin' the old .22 rifle, I went to work. After plucking, cleaning and dismembering all three, taking care to save out the hearts, livers and gizzards to grace the creamy giblet gravy I planned, I went to the kitchen. If I had any concern about the gawky, sinewy bodies that looked like they'd just spent a year furiously exercising in a fashion model fat farm, it didn't register.

I dipped the fragments in an egg and milk batter I'd seen my mother use, and then rolled them in flour laced with just a hint of garlic, and a touch of salt and pepper. Yummy. Then, it was into the hot grease to bring the battered coating to a beautiful golden brown. Periodically I jammed a fork into a meaty part to check the progress. Hmm, I thought, I must be hitting the bone. Such is the power of self-deception.

With great fanfare, I placed the platter of dark, dark, *dark* brown chicken, lumpy gravy with little stones that used to be giblets and runny mashed potatoes in front of my family and our guest, the lady who owned the pig farm.

Scientists tell us that, over eons, fossil bones turn to rock, right? On my seventy-five-cent bargain fossils, *everything* had turned to rock. You could have chewed through the tabletop easier than on the drumstick of one of these birds. What hurt worse was that the tabletop may have tasted better to boot! Speaking of taste, the order-in pizza was pretty good that night and with enough wine, memories of the disaster faded quickly.

The next day, I took the leftovers to the monkeys' cages. Three days later they were still gnawing on them without any discernible progress. I think the landlady took them out, fearing they would wear their teeth down to a point where she'd have to put them on a special diet of gruel.

I never became a gentleman farmer and my recipe for *'Russell Fried Chicken'* never inspired a cooking show on TV but I did learn one thing: those monkeys weren't that darn tough.

33

WHiLe PLoWed, our PregNaNt Pig Produced a Passel of Plastered Porkers

I've been told I come from farming stock. You couldn't prove it by me. My grandparents on my mother's side hailed from Mississippi and Arkansas. Mom, along with three brothers and four sisters, were raised on a farm. Pop was brought up in a little farming community in northern Texas. With all this background you would think I would have at least an inkling of animal husbandry and things agrarian. You'd be wrong. I don't know diddly-squat about that stuff.

That sets the stage for the bizarre tale of my one and only foray into what might be laughingly called ranching. We moved onto two-and-a-half acres in the high desert of California, north of Los Angeles. During the day I worked for an air conditioning and refrigeration company. That left my nights and weekends free. A neighbor had piglets for sale. To move the story along, we bought one. The neighbor instructed us on what to feed it, what kind of pen to build and how long it would take to fatten it up for slaughter. Additionally, she cautioned, "Don't name it, don't pet it, don't talk to it, just feed it. In a wink, I was a rancher with a herd of one … pig.

Since I worked during the day, the burden of feeding and caring for the beast was left to my wife. Before the week was out, Mimi had a name. That's a big no-no if you're raising food. Not only that, I was informed she would come when she was called and she loved to have her belly rubbed. As I found out later, that trick only worked if there was the promise of food. You can probably see where this is going.

Soon I heard, "Can't we keep Mimi as a breeder? And then we can sell the piglets. You don't want to kill her, do you? Please, please, pulleeeease, can we keep her?" Scrooge himself would have had a hard time keeping a dry eye after that guilt trip. Mimi was in, ham steaks were out. Life settled into a routine with us on a diet because Mimi was consuming huge amounts of our food budget. I've never seen anything eat like that. Well, there was this one kid in high school, but that's another story.

Weeks went by and Mimi grew and grew and grew. At last she entered puberty with all its biological and psychological changes. We called the neighbor, gave her the symptoms and she proclaimed Mimi ready for motherhood. With the help of ten pounds of carrots and who knows how many grapes, I coaxed her into the back of the pickup and carted her to the neighbors to visit her waiting suitor, a boar named Bubba. Mimi showed no reluctance at all to enter the pen with that brute. As I stood slack-jawed watching her in action I could see why. I felt color rising in my cheeks. What a trollop. I was embarrassed that a female I'd raised from practically a baby could act in such a wanton fashion. I was only glad her mother wasn't there to see such a spectacle. What am I talking about, her mother was probably just as bad.

Luring Mimi back into the truck for the trip home was a little more problematic because it was apparent she didn't want to leave. Once home, life settled down again, but a few months later we were confronted by a new set of problems. Neither of us had ever had anything to do with the birth of a pig. What does one look for, how does one go about it? We placed another call to the neighbor.

"Keep an eye on her. She'll let you know when she's ready. She'll act kind of strange and dig out a hole in her pen. You'll know it's going to happen that night. Don't feed her until evening, then mix vodka into her food and wait." She told us what to do after the birth, such as snipping off the canine teeth and some other stuff but mostly we should let her take care of everything.

I prepared Mimi's evening meal and, to be honest, the neighbor didn't tell me how much vodka to put in her food so I dumped in the whole bottle. It was a happy pig that flopped down in her nest hole that night. The first piglet came at about eleven o'clock. I was watching from outside the fence while my wife played midwife. Mimi snorted, let out a large grunt and squirted the darn thing across the pen, like skipping a pebble across the water. After a few seconds, she raised up, looked back to see what all the commotion was about, let out a large belch and, with a snort, flopped back into her alcohol-induced coma. By twelve o'clock it was all over and we stumbled off to bed, leaving eight little porkers feeding happily on their mother's 80-proof milk.

Some months later I took a job in Las Vegas and we gave Mimi to friends with the proviso she not become pork chops or bacon. My wife told them her name was Mimi and she came when she was called and she liked to have her belly rubbed. I noticed she didn't add that Mimi also enjoyed a cocktail of an evening. No sense telling them about the undue burden we were about to put on their liquor bill.

34

MoNa, a ReaL K-9 CoN Artist

I had been dog-less since Duchess passed on in early 1959. Then in 1961 I adopted a beautiful German shepherd puppy I named Mona II, after the dog we lost in the attack on Pearl Harbor. A couple of weeks after the attack, that dog was found hiding in a Hawaiian sugar cane field by the Humane Society and shipped to us a month later. If you remember, in the story "Do Kids Need Dogs? You Bet!" (*Plainsman*, August 30, 2014), she was so traumatized by the explosions and bombing, she became paranoid and skittish after we got her back and we finally had to have her put down. Any little noise caused her to run, seeking a hiding place or driving her into doggie hysterics. (Psychoanalytic therapy for dogs was unheard of in 1942.)

At any rate, in 1961, while driving in the backcountry of southern California, I came across a sign in front of a farm advertising German shepherd puppies for sale and I decided to drop in, 'just to have a look.' That's all I was going to do … just have a look. When I first saw her, she was a rambunctious little ball of fur crawling over the top of her littermates to get to me. She looked like a stuffed toy you'd buy the kids, and from the moment I saw her I knew I had to have her.

Mona was a jewel from the start and became my constant companion. Three or four months later, while driving on a country road near a lake, I stopped to let her relieve herself and run a bit. There was a patch of rocks and I picked one up and threw it, just for something to do. Mind you, I had tried numerous times to entice Mona to play ball but she showed no interest in the sport. However, she took off at a dead run and brought the rock back. I threw it again and she retrieved it once more. The silly dog didn't care to play ball, but chasing rocks, that was okay. It became our pastime. Whenever we stopped where there was an open field or space, I would find a stone and the game was on.

On one such occasion, in a clearing festooned with handy sized missiles, I selected a likely candidate and lobbed it. It landed in another patch of stones. As I watched, she took off with her ears flopping and hindquarters weaving (she was still a puppy and hadn't developed the trademark stand-up ears nor gained complete control of her hind quarters, so her back end tended to drift about), and ran to the area where the rock landed, picked it up and brought it back. Some minute detail about the casual way she approached the retrieval process put me on the alert, and I began to watch more closely.

Then, I caught her. Mona was not being honest with me. It looked like she would shilly-shally out to where she thought the rock might have landed, select a convenient substitute and bring it back. I was certain this was the way the scam worked so the next time I picked up ammunition, I looked it over before I threw it. Sure as shootin', it wasn't the same rock she dumped at my feet a moment later. I was flabbergasted, Mona, my very own dog and trusted companion, was cheating. For some moments I was crushed. I, the very soul of fair play and honesty, was cavorting with a lowly con artist, a charlatan rock retriever, a fetching phony.

However, after the initial shock receded, reason took over, and I had to admit her little flim flam scam wasn't all that serious and in fact showed real intelligence. She was getting exercise and I was getting a bit myself, so did it really matter if she brought back a different rock?

Probably not and I was content to go along with the skit until the day she introduced a new wrinkle when she went after a rock and brought back a stick. A man has to draw a line somewhere, but she was so darn cute I couldn't. If my suspicions were correct, Mona was really, P. T. Barnum reincarnated.

Perhaps, P. T. was right when he said, "There is a sucker born every minute." I suspect maybe I was one of them.

35

Why is There Never a Police Dog Around When You Need One?

A couple of years after I got Mona, I married and moved to Phoenix. As usually happens with marriage, it almost inevitably leads to the arrival of babies, in this case, two. One evening, when the girls were toddlers we called for a babysitter because we had an invitation to join friends for dinner and a movie. When our babysitter arrived, I introduced myself, and my wife, and showed the young lady the girls' room where the two were fast asleep. Mona followed and watched the process and, on several occasions, the girl patted her head and ran her hand over the dog's back. She seemed quite comfortable with Mona and we with her, so we left the bedroom door ajar and prepared to go out.

"Here's the number where we can be reached after ten and before that, call the *Bijou Theatre,* I've written the number here. There's some Cokes in the refrigerator and cookies in that jar so make yourself at home and we should be back about midnight," my wife said as we went out the door. Everything seemed 'hunky-dory', and we were looking forward to a night out in the company of adults.

Supper was wonderful and the movie hilarious. About eleven o'clock, back at the friend's house, we were just getting ready to sit down for a game of canasta when my wife asked to use the phone and excused herself. A few moments later, she came back into the room with a funny look on her face.

"Everything alright?' I asked.

"Huh … yeah, apparently, but I think next time we better leave Mona outside."

"Why?" I asked, a bit of surprise registering in my voice.

"Because I asked the babysitter how the girls were and she said, 'How should I know, that darned dog won't let me down the hall.'"

"You want to go home?"

"Maybe we better. The poor girl said Mona wouldn't let her get to the bathroom either. (That door was right next to the girls' bedroom.) What if there's a fire?"

"Good point."

When we arrived home, both Mona and the babysitter were glad to see us. Mona, because she was always glad to see us, and the babysitter because her bladder was about to explode. After that episode, we used the girl on several other occasions without any trouble. Our secret? When we went out, so did Mona.

Some weeks later, my sister-in-law was visiting. My brother would be over later after work, so we were sitting in the carport in the late afternoon having a cocktail. I was drinking beer in a heavy glass mug. The girls were occupied with dolls and a dollhouse while Mona was among them, supervising. A few moments later, I watched as a car came around the corner at the end of the block and stopped.

It was what we called a 'low rider' so I knew it was kids. There were four of them and after the driver revved the engine up a couple of times, he floored it and popped the clutch, laying about sixty-foot strips of rubber and producing a cloud of blue smoke.

By the time he got to our house he had to be doing better than forty and I jumped up, grabbed the beer mug and let fly. I had to lead them by a couple of car lengths, and when the mug hit the street, it shattered into a thousand pieces and sprayed the whole side of the car. They stopped, struggled to make a u-turn, (no easy task with a car sitting so low to the ground) and came back. I was waiting for them.

The driver's window was down, and he growled, "You throw something at my car, man?"

"You bet I did. If I ever see you coming up my street like that again I'm going to be throwing a lot more than a glass."

"We weren't hurtin' nothin', man."

"My girls cross this road to play with the neighbors and if one of them ever winds up on the front end of your stupid car, I'm comin' after you. You drive slow through here, got it?" It was tough talk I maybe couldn't back up, but I was mad.

They grumbled some obscenities, dumped it, laid another strip and drove away, flagging me the bird as they did.

When I got back to the carport, I was thoroughly shaken. After a moment I asked, "Where was Mona?"

"Oh," said my sister-in-law, "I was holding her here to keep her out of the way."

"What? I'm out there facing four teenage brutes and you're holding my eighty-pound German shepherd here? I want them to see her, I want them to know I have her."

"Oh, sorry, I didn't think about that."

It was lucky those were only kids in the car that night or I might have really gotten my clock cleaned.

36

AH, Nature!

I built a birdhouse this winter, a very special birdhouse with no back wall. I was determined that my wife Norelle and I were going to watch the miracle of birth and commune with nature from the comfort of our home. I crafted it carefully, paying attention to each detail. After construction, I painted it, installed a solar light so we could see what goes on inside during the night. At the first inkling of spring, I mounted it on a window with silicone glue. *Ta Dah!* It was magnificent.

My plan was to tape a piece of cardboard or paper with a peephole on the inner window so we could view the happenings in the nest without the mother bird seeing us. It was at this point the project began to hit some snags. In my design, I hadn't factored in that windows back here are storm type (What do I know, I'm from California). That left a gaping hole between the open back of the birdhouse outside and the cardboard on the inner window. The design flaw meant the bird could peek obliquely and view the happenings inside our little nest without us seeing her. I had to cut a much bigger piece of cardboard.

That night, I checked through the peephole and wow, the solar light was almost blinding. It was like broad daylight in that little cubbyhole. Of course, that may present some slight discomfort to the birds but no matter, it should enhance the photographic record I was planning to keep of the births. Now, with a feeder hanging close by and the warm days of spring upon us, all I had to do was wait.

I was anticipating I might have to referee one or two arguments over which avian tenant saw it first and was ready to move in. What I didn't anticipate was waiting, and waiting, and waiting. Those flighty little feather dusters didn't mind eating the food I put out, but did they check out the neighborhood, *noooo*. I watched with growing frustration as one after another gorged and flew off, never even looking at the beautiful little cottage barely two feet away.

In desperation, I decided to advertise. Maybe they were unaware of my generous offer. I put a sign by the little front door, 'Spacious efficiency apartment. Move in at once. No rent.' Still, no takers, so I added, 'No utilities'. That should have done something … it didn't. At the end of a week, I decided to really up the ante. I threw a few twigs and dried up blades of grass inside and scrawled the word 'furnished' at the bottom of the sign, all to no avail.

In the meantime, Norelle, with the sharp eye of an outdoorsman, pointed out how my creation was blocking our view out the back window. There better be some action soon or to preserve my household harmony, I was going to have to demolish it and settle for the *Nature Channel* on TV. Boy, I never knew birds could be such ingrates, although I should have. I've parked under a few overhanging branches and had to clean their love offerings off the windshield before.

37
Clip Joint or I Can't Move 'Cause I'm Stuffed

The little white cottage attached to the back window is still vacant, in spite of my efforts to find suitable tenants. If you remember my article in April, I told of building a birdhouse with no rear wall and gluing it to the window facing our back yard. I hoped it would attract a nesting mother so Norelle and I could watch the motherly activities when the eggs started hatching. In all this time, not one bird stepped up to the plate, even though, as an incentive, I hung a feeder right next door to the darn thing.

None stopped to savor the comfort and sturdy support of the perch sticking out under the generous front opening. Nor did even one avian wanderer stop to look inside at the sumptuous interior and spacious floor plan. I'm beginning to think South Dakota birds have no sense of style, no flair for gracious living and so I resigned myself to watching the pretty little house fall into disrepair and decline as time pressed on.

Then, the other day, I happened to look up from my desk and my eye fell on a sight I had longed to see for weeks, a bird. It was astraddle the perch and peeking in the front door of my little birdhouse. I didn't actually see it look inside but it was logical to assume it did. You can't imagine my thrill as I rose slowly from my desk to look closer. My long distance spectacles were in the car and for just a second I thought about going to fetch them. But there was no time – my little prospective tenant might move on, so I crept past the window and slipped out the side door.

My visitor didn't move and I thought, *He's struck by the sturdiness of the construction and the quality paint job. Here's a bird that appreciates the finer things.* At the back of the house, I paused and, after taking a deep breath, I peeked around the corner. He was still there. What a steadfast and determined individual he was. I remember thinking, *he's obviously discerning, intelligent, and not the least bit flighty.* These are all pluses in a prospective tenant.

Not wanting to startle him, I ambled slowly to the garage and stood for a moment in its shadow before venturing out onto the lawn. My remarkable little visitor, showing real pluck, held steady. My admiration soared. *I wish he'd turn my way,* I thought, so I can better see him. I decided to step closer.

"Steady, little fella, I'm not going to hurt you," I mumbled as I closed the distance between us. He still didn't move or look at me. There was something odd about him. He had not changed position since I first saw him. I moved closer, then closer. "What is that where his feet are supposed to be?" I said under my breath. "It looks like a plastic clip… Wait a minute, it *is* a plastic clip." I could see he was clipped to the perch. "This bird is a fake!"

With that discovery, I felt betrayed and victimized, but there was something else … I think I was red-faced, too. I stood up straight and glanced around the fence line to make sure no one was watching me. Of course, with my eyesight, I probably wouldn't have known if there was anyone there anyway.

Later, the mystery was solved when Norelle confessed she'd come across the bird in her things, put it there to jazz up the front entrance and forgot to tell me. Since then we've added a phony nest, with phony eggs and another phony bird to sit on them. It would be nice if they hatched and we had some phony chicks to watch too.

38

Visitor's Day and the Would-Be Warrior

In 1953, while the Korean War was winding down, I joined the Marines. I envisioned myself in that beautiful dress-blue uniform doing all sorts of heroic things. Alas, I was killed twice in boot camp war games so it's a good thing I never got over there. They signed the cease fire a month after I enlisted. Boot camp, at the time, was an ordeal in which the recruit was locked up for twelve weeks of intensely intense indoctrination by professional bullies. One was literally torn down and rebuilt from the ground up into the material the Marines were looking for. However, there was at least one break from the incessant madness and mind-numbing physical exertion. As I remember, that came in the second month, and it was called Visitor's Day.

Families who could, (I was lucky, my family lived in San Diego), trooped in on a sunny Sunday morning, eager to see if their favored son was being properly cared for. What a rude shock it must have been for them to see Johnny for the first time since he'd enlisted. Picture them all standing around, expectant and excited to see their gallant adventurer. Then picture Johnny arriving, with a teensy weensy little bit of hair struggling to cover his bare scalp and two big bushy eyebrows. (All this time they thought he had wavy hair, now it turns out the lad's hair was straight, it was his head that was wavy.)

Instead of the girlfriend and relatives getting to see their dashing hero in uniform, they see what looks like an escapee from a Georgia chain gang acting like something from another planet. Dressed in fatigues buttoned to the throat and hanging like rags because of all the weight he's lost, he cowers in the bushes, trying to be invisible. He was neither the ne're-do-well flibbertigibbet that a few weeks earlier seemed permanently attached to the refrigerator door handle, nor the stalwart, steely-eyed warrior they were expecting to find. Still, in his defense, he was a work in progress and to display him in public at that time might have been a bit counterproductive.

"Johnny, what are you doing? Come out here so we can see you. Why are you acting so strange?"

Casting furtive glances around, expecting an explosion from somewhere if he lets go and acts like a human, Private John Creepy edges out from his hiding place, grabs a peanut butter sandwich and then dives back into the bush to wolf it down.

"Oh my goodness, what's happened to you?" The mother is staggered to see the precious life she brought into the world and nurtured all these years is in such pitiful state. The father, of course, always knew the kid would probably wind up no good.

"Johnny, Johnny, you look terrible. What are they doing to you? I'm going to see the general right now."

"No, no, Mom, don't do that. Pleeese, don't do that!"

I'm still not sure, even at this writing, if visiting a recruit is a wise idea. It's like the artist showing his masterpiece when it's only half finished. Believe me, at that time, we were really half-baked. One must take pause and wonder at the wisdom of such a program. No one really comes away assured. Not the mother, who sees her son reduced to a quivering skeleton hiding in the bushes. Not the girlfriend, who's now thinking twice about what she's about to get into. Certainly not the recruit who, in a few moments, must return from this fantasy world of hugs, laughter and peanut butter sandwiches to the shrieking, snarling world of drill instructors and the daily grind.

Visitation is, no doubt, a concession to the mothers. It is a ploy to keep them from storming the gates, enraged by the offspring's letters describing the terrible conditions suffered at the hands of the Corps. By now, all who are on the mailing list know about the maggoty food, daily beatings, lack of sleep, and the nonexistent sanitation. A young mind, trying to impress someone with how tough he's got it, can conjure up stories of hardship that would make Joseph Stalin or Kim il Sung drool with delight. Maybe one like the following:

dear mom, i only got a minit to rite. there taking us out on a five hundered mile hike soon. i dont now when we'll be back. but dont worry, cause theyre feeding us ok now that fly season is over. yesterday we had to swim to catalina with a full pak and all our gear and only two of the guys had to be resqued frum dronding. the drill instructer said we'll pobably go strate into combat when we get out of here. after all mom, that is wat were traned for, to be killers.

yure sun billy
    P.s. say good bye to little joey and spot for me.

You can imagine the earful the general would have gotten after a mother read this. The Marine Corps had a tactic to combat such creative letter writing. The drill instructors merely ran us until we were too exhausted to write. It made things easier on everyone − except, that is, the recruit. Ah, those were the days. *Gung-Ho, Semper Fi* and all that.

39

Where a Bull Session Really is all About Bulls

I was raised out west and mucked around in big cities and on the desert all my life. Three years ago, I met and married one of your fabulous South Dakota women and moved to Huron. It follows that my knowledge of flora, fauna and things agricultural ranks right up there with my insight into quantum physics and rocket science … that is to say, zip-0. One's self-esteem can really take a hit back here if the biggest herd one ever raised was a few scraggly rabbits in a backyard hutch, and the only plant nurtured with any success was a weed.

The other night we had dinner with two other couples and I was seated between a pair of farmers/ranchers. They were yakking about subjects that could have been real fascinating in Hooterville or Mayberry, and maybe even relevant. It wasn't that I couldn't get a word in edgewise, heck, I didn't have any sort of word to stick in there. These guys could have been talking in Zimbabwean gibberish and I wouldn't have known the difference. I didn't understand any of it. Actually, it was kind of comforting, to be able to sit quietly, because my mother always admonished me to remember the old adage: 'It's better to sit quietly and be thought a fool than to open your mouth and remove all doubt'.

When the evening was over, I left feeling a bit inadequate. In a few moments, however, I brightened when the thought came to me that I knew a few things these guys didn't. For instance, I'll bet neither one of 'em can tell the difference between a *Joshua tree* and a *creosote bush*, and how come nothing grows around creosote bushes? Also, how about identifying a slider and a boomer and which one gives the better ride? Tell me that, Mr. Cowman and while you're at it, how many trout does it take to change a light bulb? (I threw that one in to see if you were awake.)

Getting back to my self-analysis, I rode that train of thought further. I wondered if either of them had ever competed with sixty-seven thousand other cars for the same parking spot or bounced around in a tall building during an earthquake. Finding the whole process very enabling, I tried to think of more things I might know that they didn't. Then I came up with the ultimate zinger and I sat smugly basking in its brilliance. I knew they didn't know that I knew that they didn't know what I knew. I'm feeling a lot better now... I think.

40

It's Christmas so Some Re-assembly May be Required

In Phoenix, it seldom snows on Christmas. It fact, being in the desert it hardly snows at all and I only saw it happen once in eight years. It is also rare if the temperature falls below freezing at night. Thus, with light protection, a person could work outdoors even in late December. Keeping this in mind, let me tell you a Christmas story guaranteed to bring a tear to the eye of even the most hardened holiday cynic. In 1971, my wife and I were out one evening shopping for a Santa gift our two girls.

In the outdoor playground section of a large department store I said, "Hey, look at this one! Whatdaya think?"

"Oh, my goodness, it's so big. It's going to take up the whole back yard."

"I know, but the girls will love it. Look, it has four swings so they can have their friends over and they can all swing without arguing about it. It'll be great."

"You don't think something smaller will do?"

"Yeah, but the smaller ones don't have the patented *Super Sonic Teeter-Totter* and *Cork-Screw Slide*, and that's a good price for this baby," I said, pointing. "Let's do it."

"Well … okay, if you think we should."

"It's Christmas, honey. Where's your spirit? Miss! Miss, we'll take one of these."

I lugged the box home on top of the old station wagon and the weight bottomed out the springs. That should have been a warning but I chose to ignore the signs. I almost got a hernia carrying the thing from the car into the garage. There I covered it in a tarp and piled some boxes and stuff on top.

A week later, on the afternoon of Christmas Eve, I was in the kitchen taking inventory in preparation for the night's festivities. "Let's see: one dozen eggs separated, a gallon of milk, one quart whipping cream, vanilla, sugar, a fifth of bourbon, a pint of brandy and a pint of rum and nutmeg. Good, now to whip up the egg whites and cream the yolks. I should have this ready about the time people start arriving."

Later, that evening, with the kids in bed, the company gone and after a full meal and seven or eight eggnogs under my belt, the first yawn tugged at my mouth. In a word, I was mellow.

My wife broke up my euphoria with, "Honey, don't forget you have to set up Santa's gift."

"Oh, yeah," I groaned, "I forgot about that. Can't we just give it to them in a box and say Santa didn't have time to put it together?"

The look from the kitchen would have made Adolph Hitler cringe in self-loathing and the words themselves were coated with an inch of ice. "I suppose, if you think that would be the thing to do. I think they'll be awfully disappointed, but you do what you think best and don't worry about their feelings."

"Okay, okay, I'm going," I grumbled, pushing myself up out of my easy chair.

"Let's see," I mumbled, holding the half-inch-thick instruction book under the back porch light and straining my eyes to read, "Placing main support bar, part number 7A32.670-A1/37.33 (Quantity 1) on the ground, place an end cap, part number 7A34.482-B7/42.65 (Quantity 4) on each end and attach with six (6) part number 7A37.863-A14/35.873 screws (Quantity 87). See parts list.). "Good grief, do all these screws go in this one swing set?" I mumbled, before reading on. "Pre-assemble assembly number A35.207/18EZ-302 (Quantity 6) by holding stabilizing bracket, part number 8A39.383-…. Where was this novel written?" I turned to the front cover. "Oh, Bangladesh. I might have known." And so it went for the next two torturous hours. "Boy," I grumbled, picking up an A36.402/16PB-784A (Quantity 8) stabilizer and thrust bracket, and rooting around for 7A37.863-A14/35.876 (Quantity 38) screws, "I don't believe it took this many screws to build the *Titanic*."

When the last screw was installed in the last screw hole I could find, there was still a gob of 7A37.863-A14/35.876 screws left over. I surmised they made a mistake at the factory. Now, with the massive structure looming in the gloom of the early morning darkness, I dragged my exhausted body inside and crawled between the sheets.

"Did you get it done?" my wife woke up long enough to ask.

"I hope so. Next year we buy pre-assembled…, did you hear me?"

"Zzzz."

A few hours later, in the grey mists of dawn when nothing should be stirring, a little voice began to encroach on the swirling nothingness of my slumber. "Daddy, Daddy, the slide fell off the new swing set…. Daddy?"

I was just dreaming that a giant 7A37.863-A14/35.873 (Quantity 87) screw had fallen out of the 7A34.482-B7/42.65 (Quantity 4) end cap and was pinning me to the ground when out of the fog the little voice intruded again, "Please, Daddy, get up, it's my turn to slide."

This is a nightmare, I thought, I *don't care what it costs, next year's Santa gift will be preassembled and delivered - period.* Then, through the turbulent haze of sleep deprivation and self-pity caused by overindulgence came a much more tantalizing line of speculation, *I wonder if there's any eggnog left?*

"Daddy."

"Okay, okay, I'm getting up."

"Hurry, Daddy, you need you to put the teeter-totter seat back on too."

41

Hard Lessons For a California Transplant

The other day we had our 1998 Ford Explorer in for service. Along with an oil change and lube, they filled all the fluid reservoirs. That night I joined Spike Nelson and others in judging Christmas trees at a local hotel. Afterwards, some of us went to a popular watering hole downtown to grab a bite and something to drink. The temperature outside was darned cold when I left an hour later. I started Ole Betsy and nudged out onto the street.

When I pulled up to the stop sign on Dakota Avenue at 2nd Street heading west, the glare of the downtown lights showed me a covering of dust on the windshield. No problem I thought, I had a brand new batch of windshield washer fluid to take care of that situation. Smugly I pushed the button and out came the spray, flooding the windshield with fluid for the wiper blades to squeegee away along with the dirt. For a second, as I crossed the main drag, it worked like a charm and the windshield was crystal-clear and sparkling clean.

Then suddenly, half way across, like a scene out of my worst nightmare, it glazed over into a sheet of opaque grey and I was encapsulated in a smothering cocoon of frost. My only viewing options were the side and rear windows. I didn't think fast enough to look out through the sunroof. Good thing - we don't have a sunroof. Everything in front of me was a blur and although nothing was coming up behind, stopping in the middle of Second Street at Dakota Avenue didn't seem like a smart option.

I had noticed right before the 'fog out' that there was no one parked along the curb ahead of me so I took a chance and eased over. I felt the tire nudge the curb and I stepped on the brake. Four or five minutes later, when the car finally warmed up and the defroster worked again, I wheeled once more toward home, a bit wiser. I'd learned a valuable South Dakota lesson: don't use your windshield washers when it's twenty-four degrees outside. In my defense, the concept never came up in my seventy-five years of living in Southern California or the deserts of the Southwest. Now, I don't think I'll be forgetting it.

Moving along, I'd like to share another adventure wherein I try my hand at planting - again. (To remind the reader of my success rate in this field, I refer you to the *Plainsman* and three articles named "Horticultural Horrors 1, 2 and 3," dated June 13th, 28th and July 23rd. They tell it all.)

This time, though, I was almost guaranteed success because everything I needed came in a kit. My wife brought it home and, following the instructions to the letter, I planted it. (Usually I only look at the instructions after I've botched up whatever it is I'm attempting to do and have no other recourse.) I poured the soil in the pot, covered the bulb to the precise level called for and added water.

The very next day, two little nubs appeared on the top of the bulb. I had to check it twice to make sure I wasn't seeing things. In the days that followed, these things began to grow. Let me repeat that... these things began to grow. A half inch the first day, then another, and later a full two inches in a day. I calculated that in about thirty days or so, it would reach the ceiling and there would be no stopping it short of an anti-growth hormone or an ax.

To add to my concern I heard strange noises in close proximity to the darned thing. Like someone rubbing a balloon with damp fingers. I think it was the sound of cells multiplying. I had definite apprehension about letting the great grandchildren get too near for fear they'd be swallowed up. I'd read about blood-sucking plants and plants that kill animals for a living and I'm not sure of the genius here. The box called it an *Amaryllis* but was it really?

"Well, it's time to get my whip, gun and chair, I have to feed it another ration... Back, BACK YOU BEAST. Let go of my arm. Let go...HELP!" (I just added that last part for dramatic effect. I think I can still whip the darned thing if I have to.)

42

Flatlander Boot Camp

I've been told I'm a little slow on the uptake and I've even been accused by close friends – and once in a while by total strangers – of being 'out to lunch'. I must admit, some of that may be true. However, since moving here from California four years ago I've gotten a real education. It was an eye-opener and I was totally unprepared for many of the changes I walked into, a few of which I will enumerate here:

I knew I was no longer in California when…

… people told me that thirty degrees outside was actually the low end of the comfort zone.

…I found out USD didn't mean the University of San Diego.

…one runs the risk of frostbite in the morning just washing one's hands.

…I went out for a steak dinner and didn't have to rob a bank to pay for it.

…I found out it took longer to dress to go somewhere in winter than it did to get there.

…I showed up at six o'clock for a dinner date and found out I was about six hours late, but
just in time for supper.

…I found out I had to go through two doors to get into a house and two to get out.

…I had to scrape ice rather than seagull droppings off the windshield, pre-warm the car so the skin on my hands wouldn't stick to the steering wheel, and apply the brakes two hundred yards ahead of where I would have normally when approaching a stop sign.

...I first started hearing phrases like 'white out, tornado warning, black ice,' and saw people skating around on the sidewalks – without any skates.

...only five cars on the same street constituted a traffic jam.

...I found out the majority of people go to church on Sunday and not the beach.

...that all those silly people who looked like they were out cutting their lawns in the dead of winter were actually running snow blowers.

...I spent an hour looking for a city called 'Pier' on a map of South Dakota.

Finally, I knew I was no longer in California when I found out people didn't pay much attention to the wind until it had chunks of houses or cattle in it.

It hasn't been all bad though. I found out trees do beautiful things with their leaves in the fall and the hardest water in the world was not in Death Valley but right on my doorstep in January. It's called ice. (Of course, you don't see much of that in Death Valley.) All and all, I fell in love with South Dakota and, oh yeah, a special woman who lived there.

43

Maiden Flight of an Aerial Sodbuster

A lot of years ago, for my nephew's birthday, I bought him a gas-powered *Stuka* dive-bomber model airplane. It was one of those kind tethered by strings you fly in circles. The fact that it was built of plastic, pre-assembled and durable was important. The kid was known to be a little hard on toys.

Anyway, this thing intrigued me. I was kind of an airplane nut and here was this beautiful little scale model, all shiny, and looking like the real thing. I hated what the Nazis did with them but that wasn't the fault of the airplane. I imagined myself in front of the screaming crowds doing loop-the-loops and all sorts of aerobatic stunts. Of course, I would be on the ground holding the strings and going in circles, (which is natural for me), not actually flying (which is unnatural for me). I simply had to have one for myself; there was just no other option.

However, the real selling point was the preassembled business. I still had my partially- assembled plastic model of the clipper ship, *Cutty Sark*, and a lot of the pieces (at least I think there were still a lot of the pieces) sitting in a box in the tool shed. One of my yearly New Year's resolutions was, 'I'd get back to it someday.' That was three years before (you can see how well that was working out). So, it was back to the store from whence I bought the thing, in search of my own *Stuka*.

When I got it home, I put all the little printed plastic decals on the wings and fuselage, then attached the strings. The handle, however, had an interesting feature. It was a series of holes where you tied the strings. The instructions said (I don't remember the exact wording because I usually only glance at those things anyway) something to the effect that beginners should use the holes in the middle and then work their way out as they gained experience. *Oh, piffle,* I thought, *I know a lot about airplanes. I've watched guys fly these things and I've seen a lot of movies,* so, I promptly attached the strings to the two outer-most holes so I could really maneuver this baby.

The guy next door, a loud, outspoken truck driver and his equally boisterous son, saw me in the carport and came over to see what I was up to. "What are you doing, neighbor?"

"Oh, hi, Jim, Mike. I was just about to go down to the schoolyard and fly my new model airplane. Wanna come along?"

"Sure, let me grab a cup of coffee and I'll be right with you."

I was thinking, as I loaded my prize in the back seat of our car, *Oh, boy, an audience, and a helper.* Up until then, I wasn't sure how I was going to start the engine and then run to the controls before the plane got off the ground.

At the school yard, I set up the model, laid out the strings and control handle and when everything was set, squirted a bit of fuel in the intake on the little engine and spun the propeller. The blamed thing started right up. *Man,*

I thought, *this is going to be easier than I imagined.* With Jim holding the roaring beast by its tail, I scurried over, picked up the controls and, when I was set, signaled him to let go.

Remember that thing about the holes on the control handle and where to put the strings if you're a beginner? You, know, the ones I ignored. Too bad I didn't have a moment to read them again, but there was only maybe a split second before catastrophe struck and there just wasn't enough time. That whining little rocket jumped off the ground, flew level at about ten inches altitude for maybe two feet, turned pure vertical and in a beautiful swooping arc, went right over my head and at warp speed, straight into the ground. After the terrible 'krumping' noise, earth shaking tremors and massive dust cloud cleared, there was a dead silence.

Without a word, I picked up the box, scooped up the wreckage and headed for the car. The silence continued during the ride home and the walk to the back door. My neighbors tagged along behind like puppy dogs. It was all very reverent. I suspect they were just curious as to what my excuse was going to be. I opened the door, held the box out, and said to my wife, "Light the sacrificial candle."

It must have been too much drama for Jim and Mike because they collapsed in gales of laughter in the driveway. They had been holding it in all the way from the crash site to the house. It was later Jim confessed, because he didn't know me very well at the time, that he had whispered to Mike, "Don't you laugh or say a word." He was unsure what my reaction to the disaster was going to be. Once they found out, there was no stopping the merriment. The story was told and retold around the neighborhood and I caught people pointing at me and whispering behind their hand.

I never bought another *Stuka* or tried my hand at aerobatics again, and even though that flight was spectacular (then again, so was the *Hindenburg's*), I find myself wishing it could have lasted just a little bit longer. Who knows, I might have had some fun.

The end

Other books by Bill Russell

China Clipper – With the vast Pacific Ocean and exotic tropical islands as a backdrop, this story of love, danger and adventure invites the reader into a world long gone. In 1937, Pan American Airway's fabulous new seaplane, *China Clipper*, roared off the waters of San Francisco Bay, and headed across the Pacific to the Philippines. Among the passengers was a pretty heiress, on her way to an arranged marriage, a bodyguard hired by her father to watch over her, and a vicious kidnapper with plans to strike once they reach Manila. During the five-day island-hopping journey with overnight stays in Hawaii, Midway Atoll, Wake Island and Guam, the heiress and her bodyguard fall in love. It's a situation with consequences the would-be kidnapper could not have anticipated.

Not Without Fear – Set in the 'rough 'n tumble' Pacific Northwest at the turn of the last century, this is a story of love, hate, tenderness and triumph. Emily Britt, wife of a cruel and abusive schooner captain twice her age, finds love and solace in the arms of another, her husband's first mate. When the captain learns of her infidelity he tries to murder the mate and then increases the cruelty on Emily. When she runs, he follows with murder on his mind. However, once cornered, the captain underestimates the power of a desperate woman and fails to realize she is now much more dangerous than he.

In Lieu of Surrender – Almost everyone has made a big mistake at some time in their life. Roy Gallant, a pillar of Santa Marcia society, has just made a pip. Hiding for years behind the façade of respectability, he's up to his ears in smuggling, crooked cops, nefarious shenanigans and greed. Then, as blithely as swatting a fly, he engineers the murder of the town's young chief of police. That act invites the attentions of a private investigator, Toby Grant, who comes snooping. It turns out the victim was Toby's best friend and, although Roy doesn't realize it yet, that makes this decision his biggest boo-boo ever. Set amid the beauty of 1949 Southern California, the action plays out all the way from the high desert of Bakersfield to the orange groves of Anaheim to the pristine beaches around Santa Barbara. In reality, the whole thing might be said to have started in 1942 in the Japanese-American concentration camp near Lone Pine, California, known as *Manzanar*.

Doomed Voyage – Private Investigator Toby Grant always liked playing footsy with danger and if there was a buck to be made, so much the better. In 1950, the addition of a new wife failed to deter him from taking on a wacky assignment to transport a bunch of supposedly phony diamonds across the Pacific as a decoy for the real shipment. The threat imposed by rumors of a band of jewel thieves only added spice to the assignment in his mind. The flimsy story regarding the reason for the ruse stunk like old fish and seemed as bogus as the gems themselves. That should have made the detective run and not look back, but he had two other character flaws that were almost his undoing – an insatiable curiosity and a yen to park a new yellow convertible in his driveway. It turns out Pam, his bride, was as big a thrill-seeker as he was and willingly went along to ride shotgun. In this tale of murder, piracy, deceit, and danger on the high seas, the delivery of the gems is all but forgotten in the frantic struggle just to stay out of the jaws of death.

Your Other Left, Idiot! A hilarious memoir about the boot camp experience as told by one who went through it. Mine was in the Marines but it could be any Armed Service where the object was to *snap you out of your cheap civilian ways* and make you one of the group, be it Air Force, Navy, Army, Marines or Coast Guard. Most will agree it was a real life-changer. *(Published by The Marine Corps League, Detachment 746 of Huron, South Dakota. **All money made on the sale of this book is donated to charity.)***